C32   1950-

COLLINS

Safari Guides

Common Birds
of East Africa

Martin B. Withers & David Hosking

D0841527

HarperCollins Publishers

FOR SALLY & AMY

HarperCollins*Publishers*
77–85 Fulham Palace Road
London
W6 8JB

The HarperCollins website address is:
www.**fire**and**water**.com

Collins is a registered trademark of HarperCollins*Publishers* Ltd

10 9 8 7 6 5 4 3 2

03 02 01 00 99

ISBN 0 00 220034 1

Colour reproduction by Colourscan, Singapore

Printed and bound by Rotolito Lombarda, Italy

ACKNOWLEDGEMENTS

There are countless people to whom the authors owe a debt of gratitude for the production of this book. They would like to express special thanks to Myles Archibald and his staff at HarperCollins. To the staff at United Touring International Ltd, London, in particular Joanne Peers, Versha Veghala, Cordelia Robb, Helen Simmans and Jonathan Bolden. To Neil Outram, General Manager United Touring Company, Arusha, Tanzania and to John Glen, General Manager United Touring Company, Nairobi, Kenya. We would like to make special mention of our drivers Joseph Nicholas Kwelukilwa, Moses Sengenge and Suleiman Kiruwa in Tanzania and Dominic Gichinga in Kenya without whose driving skills and sharp eyesight many of the illustrations featured would not have been obtained. Thanks are also due to the management and staff of the Frank Lane Picture Agency, Graham Armitage CZ Scientific Instruments Ltd, Graham Rudaford Fuji, London, Phil Ward and to all clients of Hosking Tours who have helped to make much of our time in East Africa such an enormous pleasure.

Lastly, we owe a huge thank you to our wives and families for their support and tolerance during the production of this book.

Martin B. Withers FRPS
David Hosking FRPS

PREFACE

The main objective of this book is to provide visitors to East Africa with a guide to the birds most likely to be encountered during the course of a safari in and around the main National Parks and Game Reserves of Kenya, Tanzania and Uganda, although many of the species featured are also commonly found in adjacent countries. It was not our intention to produce complete coverage of the birds of East Africa. The species included in this edition were selected based on the personal experiences of the authors, gained during visits to the region over a period of almost twenty years. Anyone wishing to obtain greater and more detailed information on species should consult the bibliography.

An attempt has been made to provide as full a diagnostic description of each species featured as space would permit. In most cases this information enables the species to be identified by size, plumage colour and shape. It should be remembered that in many species plumage variations can be quite marked as a result of age and the sex of the species. We have attempted wherever possible to bring this to the attention of the reader.

A TRAVELLERS GUIDE TO
SAFARI PHOTOGRAPHY

Before your Departure

As a general rule it is unwise to commence a photographic safari with any untested equipment. Always put at least one roll of film through a new camera and carry out a full test on any newly purchased or untried lens. You should also endeavour to familiarise yourself with the use and functions of all equipment, accessories and film stock prior to your departure.

Time spent researching the areas you will be visiting can prove invaluable and, having established the flora and fauna you are likely to encounter, will aid you in selecting the most appropriate equipment to satisfy your own photographic needs.

It is also good practice to check that you have adequate insurance cover for all your equipment. Ensure that your policy fully covers equipment for loss or damage in all the countries you plan to visit and for the duration of your tour.

WHAT TO TAKE

Cameras

The choice of cameras available these days is vast. For really successful safari photographs a top brand Single Lens Reflex (SLR) camera with an interchangeable lens facility is ideal. Many of today's top models have an autofocus facility which is a great asset to the wildlife photographer. This system can save valuable seconds and consequently secure pictures that may have been missed with manual focus equipment. Due to the rigours and stresses that any safari places on equipment, we strongly advise you to take at least two camera bodies - there will be little or no chance of getting any camera repairs undertaken outside major cities. It is obviously beneficial to have two identical camera bodies, but if this is not feasible you should ensure that your 'back up' camera accepts the same range of lenses and accessories as your principle camera body. For all round versatility and ease of use the 35mm format is by far the best. Medium format cameras, using 120 film are also ideal, but these generally demand greater photographic skills of the operator than does 35mm. Whichever format you select an important consideration is having the ability to over-ride the 'auto-settings', in order to manually adjust the aperture and speed settings. Manual adjustment will allow you to utilise fully, aperture settings to obtain full depth of field and speed settings to freeze any action. Most modern day cameras have built in motordrives which wind the film on automatically between exposures. This has the advantage over a manual wind on system of allowing you to keep your eye to the viewfinder at all times, thereby lessening the risk of missing the all important shot.

Compact cameras, often with a zoom lens, perform well and can be a useful addition to your SLR outfit. However, in many instances, the short focal length fixed or zoom lens of the compact camera is unable to secure a large enough image of wildlife subjects for satisfactory results.

Lenses

The wide variety of photographic opportunities that are presented to the photographer whilst on safari demand an equally wide range of lenses. Wide-angle lenses of between 20mm & 35mm are ideal for many landscape situations and for showing herds of animals, or flocks of birds, within their natural habitats. Short telephoto lenses of 80mm, 135mm, 180mm and 200mm are ideal for many of the larger mammals and for the more approachable bird species. For the more wary mammals and the vast majority of birds, longer telephoto lenses are required. These lenses are usually 300mm, 400mm or 500mm and, although often heavy and rather large, are essential for the more serious wildlife photographer.

Mirror lenses offer a lightweight alternative to the longer telephoto lenses, but have the drawback of a fixed aperture and occasionally produce a 'doughnut' effect to background highlights, which can be very distracting in the resulting pictures.

Many of today's longer telephoto lenses are autofocus, but those that are not require very accurate focusing owing to their very shallow depth of focus.

When purchasing a long telephoto lens some attention needs to be given to the maximum aperture or 'f' stop. This can be f2.8, f4, f5.6, f6.3, f8 or similar. The 'f' stop indicates the amount of light passing through the lens to the film, the smaller the number the larger the passage of light. Consequently the maximum aperture of any lens determines the brightness of the image in the viewfinder. This is an important factor in non-autofocus lenses when critical focusing has to be established manually - the brighter the image the easier the focusing.

Zoom Lenses

Most of today's leading wildlife photographers use a range of zoom lenses. They offer the facility for very precise framing of subjects without the need for the photographer to change position.

The most useful and versatile zoom lenses for wildlife/safari photography fall within the ranges of 28mm to 80mm and 70mm to 300mm.

Although, at least initially, zoom lenses can be more difficult to operate, they can offer the travelling photographer considerable savings in weight and bulk, by reducing the number of fixed focus lenses required. Many zoom lenses are, however, one or two stops slower than an average fixed lens of similar focal length.

Macro Lenses

The inclusion of a macro lens in your equipment bag is essential if your photographic interests are in recording close-ups of insects and flowers. The most useful macro lenses have a focal length of between 90mm and 180mm, these allow a reasonable working distance from most subjects. In our experience macro lenses of around 50mm have too short a working distance, which can disturb some subjects. This short working distance can also often cause lighting difficulties, particularly when using flash. The macro facility offered by some zoom lenses can be useful but is rather restricted and in no way matches the quality of a true macro lens.

Cheaper alternatives to a macro lens include the use of extension tubes, placed between any lens and the camera body, thereby reducing the minimum focusing distance, the use of reversing rings and the use of close-up lenses attached to the front of an existing lens.

Converters

Many wildlife photographers use converters to increase the effective focal length of their prime lenses. The most widely used converters are 1.4x and 2x, however, as well as the respective gain in focal length there are respective losses of speed of an equal factor. For example a 300mm f4 lens when coupled to a 1.4x converter becomes a 420mm f5.6, and if coupled to a 2x converter becomes a 600mm f8. When coupled with good quality prime lenses the results are usually very acceptable. We do NOT recommend converters for use with zoom lenses, as they often adversely effect definition. Do remember to purchase the best quality converter that you can afford, poor quality converters, like poor quality lenses, will give poor quality results. Also check that any converter you purchase is compatible with your lenses - some are not and they can cause quite serious problems of vignetting, resulting in the outer edges of photographs, particularly the corners, being under exposed.

Filters
We strongly recommend the use of ultra violet or skylight filters on the front of all lenses, this being a relatively cheap method of protecting the expensive end element of the lens from impact damage, rain, dust, scratches and finger marks.

We also suggest that you carry a polarising filter for use in reducing unwanted reflections and darkening blue skies in landscape pictures. The drawback to using polarising filters is the resulting loss of 2 'f' stops. Polarisers are available in both linear and circular versions. Be sure to purchase whichever one best suits your camera system as some metering and autofocus systems are apt to malfunction when fitted with the incorrect type. If, as we suggest, your lenses have ultra violet or skylight filters permanently in place, do remember to remove them before fitting the polariser, otherwise there is a strong possibility of vignetting.

Film
Whether you require negatives for prints or colour transparencies for projection, there is a vast array of film stock now available. The development of fine grain film emulsions in recent years now allows the photographer to capture super-sharp images on films ranging in speed from 25 to 400 ISO. The higher the ISO number of a given film the faster it is, or the more sensitive it is to light. It therefore follows that films with lower ISO ratings (i.e. 25 ISO) will require longer exposures than do films with higher ISO ratings (i.e. 400 ISO).

The light conditions in East Africa are usually very good, with sunshine, or at least bright conditions predominating. For these conditions we would recommend the use of films with speeds of 50 to 100 ISO. In duller conditions, or in the partial gloom of dawn and dusk, films with speeds of 200 to 400 ISO would be better employed. As well as the light conditions your choice of film should be influenced by the lenses you propose to use. Lenses with maximum apertures of f2.8 or f4 will allow the use of slower films (25 to 100 ISO) than will lenses with maximum apertures of f5.6 or f8, when faster films (200 to 400 ISO) may be required.

It is undoubtedly advantageous to familiarise yourself with the

characteristics of one particular film stock, thereby being better able to judge it's exposure latitude and other qualities. Many professional photographers tend to under or over expose their film stock by 1/3rd of a stop to suit their own particular taste. In some film types a slight under exposure increases the colour saturation, whilst in others a slight over exposure adds sparkle - it's all a matter of your own particular preference, so don't be afraid to experiment, it can make quite a difference.

How much film do you need to take? This is a question many people ask and, as a general rule, we suggest that you read through your daily itinerary and attempt to estimate your daily film requirement. Having calculated this total, double it! It is unlikely that you will take too much film, but it is highly likely you may take too little! The availability of film outside major cities is often unreliable, is usually expensive, may not have been stored in ideal conditions and may well be out of date.

Many photographic travellers express alarm at the prospect of their film being subjected to 'X ray' security checks at airports. At most major airports these days security staff either refuse or are very reluctant to hand search film stock. In our experience films of 25 to 400 ISO suffer no damage as a result of 'X ray' examination - although the cumulative effects of multi 'X ray' checks may cause problems. If you are concerned we recommend you pack your film stock in lead film bags and carry them in your hand baggage. However, some airport authorities will carry out hand searches and, in order to speed up the process, it is best to carry your films in transparent packaging. An excellent way to carry film is to utilise old slide boxes, these take 4 rolls of 35mm film, offer protection from impact and dust and their transparent lids facilitate quick hand searches.

Camera Bags

A good quality camera bag that will protect expensive camera equipment from damage, dust and rain is essential for the travelling photographer. There are many well designed camera bags on the market today, with several more recent designs taking the form of rucksacks - these are excellent particularly if you expect to have to carry your equipment any great distance. In selecting a suitable bag, resist the temptation to purchase one that is too big - you will only feel obliged to fill it! With ever tightening controls and restrictions being imposed by airlines on the size and weight of cabin baggage, the smaller the better. Waist-mounted camera and lens pouches can help to spread the load.

Camera Supports

The commonest cause of picture failure is undoubtedly lack of definition as a result of camera shake. Overcoming this problem will increase your success rate enormously. Most camera instruction manuals give details of 'How to hold your Camera' and it is well worth developing a good technique in this area, with elbows locked tightly into the body.

Whenever possible we would recommend the use of a tripod. There are many light, yet sturdy models on the market which will fit comfortably into the average suitcase or roll bag. Monopods are also a good means of steadying the camera, but they do require a little

practice. On most photographic safaris to East Africa the vast majority of filming will be undertaken from a vehicle during game drives, in most cases this precludes the use of a tripod or monopod. The best alternative for photographing from a vehicle is to employ the use of a beanbag, a very simple, but extremely effective method of camera support. Although beanbags are commercially available they are not difficult to make. All that is needed is a section of cloth or canvas sewn to form a zippered bag of around 300mm x 150mm. This can be packed in your luggage and, on arrival at your chosen destination, be filled with rice, peas or beans. When the beanbag is placed on the roof of your safari vehicle it quickly moulds around your camera and lens, forming a very efficient support.

Rifle stock and pistol grip supports allow freedom of movement when attempting to photograph moving subjects such as, animals running, or birds in flight.

If you have no option other than to hand hold your camera while shooting, you should always ensure that your shutter speed is as great or greater than the focal length of the lens in use, i.e. 50mm - 1/60th., 100mm - 1/125th., 200mm - 1/250th., 500mm - 1/500th. etc.

Flash

An electronic flashgun is well worth it's place in your camera bag, not only to record any nocturnal creatures that you may encounter, but also as a 'fill in' to soften harsh shadows during the daytime and to light any close-up macro photography. Most modern day flashguns feature TTL (Through the Lens) exposure control which will guarantee correct exposure automatically. Many of these flashguns also feature an infra-red autofocus system, which overcomes the problem of focusing in the dark. In the absence of this facility, a head-mounted torch can prove invaluable, allowing you to illuminate your chosen subject while at the same time leaving both hands free to focus manually.

Batteries

The drain on battery power by autofocus systems is far greater than that of manual focus systems. As a result you should ensure that you carry a good supply of camera and flash batteries with you. The diversity of batteries employed by differing manufacturers is enormous and, even in major cities in East Africa, the availability of batteries for your particular model may be in doubt.

The variety of electrical supplies and the variation in electrical sockets encountered on safari, can reduce the effective value of rechargeable batteries.

CARE & MAINTENANCE

As a general rule it is advisable to thoroughly check and clean all your camera bodies and lenses at the end of each day's shooting. All equipment used on safari is subject to the potentially damaging effects of sunlight, damp, rain and dust. Do remember to keep camera bags and film stock out of direct sunlight whenever possible. Dust is probably the most damaging of all, a single grain on the camera pressure plate or, in the jaws of a film cassette, can badly scratch a complete roll of film. A rubber blower brush is ideal for keeping the inside of your cameras clean, while lens elements are best cleaned with specially purchased cleaning fluid and tissues. The outer casings of both cameras and lenses can best be cleaned using an ordinary household paint brush. It is always worth having a supply of large plastic bags with you, into which you can seal your entire camera bag on the days when you are travelling from one location to another. This will greatly reduce the risk of dust entering the most sensitive parts of your cameras.

PHOTOGRAPHIC TECHNIQUES

For the most part, the secret to successful photography lies in the photographers ability to master and control several major factors - those of exposure, lighting, depth of field, definition and composition. If all these factors are successfully mastered you will be producing many pleasing pictures.

Exposure

The vast majority of modern cameras have built-in metering systems, which work to a high standard and greatly reduce the possibility of picture failure as a result of incorrect exposure. However, there are many occasions when an automatic metering system may let you down. For example when photographing white birds, or light coloured animals, against a dark background or, alternatively, dark birds or animals against a light sky or background. Under such lighting conditions knowledge in the use of +/- compensation is required. In the case of white/light subjects against dark backgrounds the metering system may well be influenced to a great extent by the dark areas, thereby over exposing your main subject. This will require you to under expose to retain detail in the important white/light subject areas. Conversely in the case of dark subjects against light skies or backgrounds, the light areas may well over influence the metering, resulting in a silhouette of the main subject. This problem will require you to over expose in order to obtain detail in the shadow or dark areas of your subject. Many present day cameras have a +/- compensation facility to aid the photographer with these awkward exposure situations. Alternatively the same result can be obtained by changing the ISO rating of the film being used, although with the advent of DX coding this may not always be possible. Whichever way you choose to compensate, do remember to cancel any over or under exposure settings before moving on to the next situation.

In cases where determining the correct exposure is in doubt, it is advisable to 'bracket' your exposures. For example if your metering system indicates an exposure of 1/60th @ f8, take one picture at this setting, then two further exposures either side of it, i.e. 1/60th @ f5.6 and 1/60th @ f11. One of the resulting exposures should produce what you require, but experience with your own equipment under these difficult conditions is the only real answer.

It should also be remembered that the exposure tolerance of transparency film is far lower than that of negative film.

Lighting

During the course of a single day in East Africa, the lighting conditions experienced can vary tremendously. The conditions experienced in the early morning are often the most pleasing, the low angle of the sun producing wonderful soft lighting, with excellent modelling of the subject. These lighting conditions are often repeated in late afternoon with the addition of a warm glow towards sunset. From late morning to mid afternoon lighting conditions can be very challenging, with the sunlight often directly overhead, resulting in rather flat lighting effects.

In most cases, standard portraits of East Africa's birds and

mammals are taken with the sunlight behind the photographer, thereby fully lighting the subject. It is always worth experimenting with other lighting arrangements, particularly side or back lighting. These lighting conditions often produce spectacular and unusual pictures of even the most common bird and mammal species.

Depth of Field

Depth of field is determined by the choice of 'f' stops available on each individual lens. In most landscape pictures, taken with wide-angle or standard lens, there is a necessity for maximum depth of field, to render as much of the foreground, middle and far distance as sharp as possible. To achieve this result, it is necessary to select a small aperture ('f' stop) of f16 or f22. This will consequently result in a slow shutter speed, so ensure you use a tripod or some other means of support, to reduce the risk of picture failure as a result of camera shake.

For individual images of birds or mammals, using longer lenses, it is often better to select a large aperture ('f' stop) of f5.6 or f4. This will result in the background being thrown well out of focus, which in turn will help to isolate your main centre of interest be it bird or mammal. The use of a large aperture ('f' stop), in these circumstances, will also help to eliminate background distractions by rendering them out of focus.

Don't forget that you can check the depth of field created by any given 'f' stop, by using the depth of field button on your camera body. This button allows you to preview the finished image and to adjust it to your own satisfaction prior to making any exposure.

Definition

The success or failure of any photograph is dependent to a great extent on definition. On the whole, modern lenses are produced to a high standard and give excellent definition, any unsharp results are usually attributable to other causes. The most frequent cause is, undoubtedly, due to camera shake during exposure (See Camera Supports). Another cause can be movement of the subject during exposure, this can be lessened to a great extent by the use of a fast shutter speed.

It is, however, worth remembering that in some instances movement of the subject during exposure can often result in a pleasing pictorial image, i.e. animals running, flocks of birds flying etc.

Composition

Unlike many elements of a photograph which are automatically undertaken by the camera itself, composition demands an active input from the photographer. It is therefore, in your own interest to be fully conversant with the factors relating to good composition.

Many newcomers to photography tend to produce all of their images in a horizontal format. Cameras work equally well when turned through 90 degrees! Do remember to fully utilise the possibilities of vertical format.

Also remember to consider changing your viewpoint on occasions, don't always photograph from a standing position, explore the possibilities of photographing a subject by kneeling or even lying on the ground. On game drives don't always photograph from the open roof of the vehicle, use the windows occasionally, it can often add impact and provide better scale to the resulting pictures.

In the case of bird or mammal portraits, having decided on your format and viewpoint, you need to concentrate on the size and placement of your subject within the picture area. Generally speaking most subjects need room to move or look into the picture space, so avoid cropping your image too tightly, unless of course it is your intention to show a close-up of the subjects head.

Try to avoid placing your subject in the centre of the picture space, instead consciously divide the space into 'thirds', both vertically and horizontally and place your main point of interest where the lines cross. Do pay attention to the line of the horizon, particularly in landscapes and keep it along the 'thirds' and, at all costs keep it level. When it comes to precise framing zoom lenses are very useful, allowing control over subject size and perspective. In some cases the size of the main subject can be quite small within the picture space, provided that the inclusion of more surroundings adds information or pictorial interest to the finished image.

By utilising a range of lenses it is often possible to secure an interesting sequence of images of a bird or mammal, i.e. 50mm showing the creature in it's habitat, 200mm or 300mm producing portraits and 500mm or 600mm depicting the head only. Sequences like these can often add variety to subsequent slide shows or print albums.

The Moment of Exposure

Having located your subject, decided on the elements of exposure, lighting and composition, when do you press the shutter? This, of

course, is very subjective but any animal or bird portrait will be greatly improved and have a 'sparkle of life' if you can make your exposure when a 'highlight' is visible in the eye of your chosen subject. This is particularly important if the eye of the subject being photographed is dark and surrounded by black fur or feather.

You should always attempt to maintain concentration when photographing any subject, remaining alert to the possibility of a yawn, scratch or wing-stretch, which may provide you with only a fleeting moment in which to capture the action.

Moving Subjects

Animals or birds 'On the Move' present the photographer with some interesting problems. Supporting the camera is a major concern as the use of a tripod of monopod is usually too restricting for this type of work. Other than hand-holding the camera, a rifle stock, or shoulder pod is probably the only option available, either way you should endeavour to use the fastest shutter speed available, to minimise the risk of camera shake. Capturing any moving bird or mammal is best accomplished by 'panning'. This technique involves moving the camera in the same direction and at the same speed as the subject and taking the picture while the camera is still moving. Any resulting pictures will have a feeling of movement, showing the subject in sharp focus with the background blurred due to the motion of the panning camera.

Getting Close to Birds and Mammals

Whilst on safari the vast majority of your photography will be undertaken from a vehicle during game drives. Many opportunities also exist for wildlife photography on foot, within the grounds of safari lodges and at specially designated areas within the National Parks and Reserves.

At many of the lodges getting close to birds is often quite easy, due to the tame nature of many species. Others, however, require some knowledge of basic 'stalking' procedures to gain a close enough approach for a worthwhile image size in the finished pictures. Avoid walking straight towards your intended subject, as this is likely to cause it to fly away, a slow angled approach is more likely to succeed. Watch your subject during your approach and should it appear concerned 'freeze' for a while until it again looks relaxed. A crouched approach during a 'stalk' can also be beneficial, the smaller you appear the less likely you are to frighten your intended subject. It is also a good idea to make use of any natural cover that the terrain may offer.

Many of the safari lodges in East Africa provide food and water for the local bird population and these feeding areas can offer good photographic opportunities. Even if the bird tables themselves are non-photogenic you can attempt to photograph birds on natural perches as they make their way to and from the feeding areas.

You should exercise considerable caution when 'stalking' mammal species, remember they are wild animals and can be extremely dangerous. Never try to tempt monkeys or baboons to come closer with food items - this is a sure way to get badly bitten.

CODE OF CONDUCT

The National Parks and Reserves of East Africa operate a strict Code of Conduct for both drivers and visitors. A short, simple list of do's and don'ts have been implemented to minimise disturbance to the birds and mammals, to lessen the impact of tourism on the environment and to ensure that all visitors experience safe and enjoyable safaris.

Please do not pressurise your driver into breaking Park regulations, you will be jeopardising his job and run the risk of expulsion from the Park.

Please keep noise to a minimum, particularly when close to animals and never leave the vehicle, sit or stand on the roof, or hang precariously from the windows.

Never discard any form of litter, apart from being unsightly it can cause serious injury or even kill animals if ingested.

Cigarettes are best avoided during game drives, the careless or accidental discarding of a match or cigarette stub can lead to uncontrollable fires, resulting in the deaths of many living creatures.

GENERAL NOTES

Many people visiting East Africa express a wish to photograph the local people. Before doing so please obtain permission and be prepared for the possibility of paying for the privilege. On no account attempt to photograph military installations or personnel.

PICTURE CREDITS

The authors would like to thank the Frank Lane Picture Agency for their assistance in the compilation of the photographs used in this book. All the photographs are by the authors with the exception of those listed below:

Wahlberg's Eagle	P. Steyn
Pallid Harrier	A.Christiansen
Little Sparrowhawk	W.T.Miller
Red-chested Cuckoo	A. & K.Riley
Alpine Swift	Silvestris
African Scimitarbill	F.Lane
Bearded Woodpecker	T.Hamblin
Red-backed Scrub Robin	J.Karmali
Grey-backed Camaroptera	M.Gore
Red-faced Crombec	F.Hartmann
Variable Sunbird	M.Gore
Beautiful Sunbird	M.Gore
Golden-breasted Bunting	R.Tidman
Cardinal Quelea	J.Karmali
Yellow-billed Oxpecker	F.Polking
Black-headed Oriole	P.Steyn
Golden-tailed Woodpecker	P.Steyn
Spectacled Weaver	N. Myburgh

BIBLIOGRAPHY

The following books are recommended for the purposes of further reference.

Brown, L.H., Urban, E.L., Newman, K., Fry, C.H. & Keith, S. *The Birds of Africa*, 4 volumes to date. Academic Press.

Brown, L.H. & Amadon, D. *Eagles, Hawks & Falcons of the World*. Country Life Books.

Cramp, S. et al., editors. *Handbook of the Birds of Europe, the Middle East & North Africa - (The Birds of the Western Palearctic)*, 9 vols. Oxford University Press.

Guggisberg, C.A.W., *Birds of East Africa*, 2 vols. Mount Kenya Sundries Ltd., Nairobi.

Mackworth-Praed, C.W. & Grant, C.H.B., *Birds of Eastern & North-Eastern Africa*. 2 vols. Longmans.

Roberts, A., *The Birds of South Africa*, revised edition by Mclachan, G.R. & Liversidge, R. The Trustees of the John Voelcker Bird Book Fund, 1977.

Serle, W., Morel, G.J. & Hartwig, W. *A Fieldguide to the Birds of West Africa*. HarperCollins.

Sinclair, I., Hockey, P., Tarboton, W., Hayman, P. and Arlott, N., *Illustrated Guide to the Birds of Southern Africa*. New Holland.

Van Perlo, B. *An Illustrated Checklist to the Birds of Eastern Africa*. HarperCollins.

Williams, J.G. & Arlott, N. *A Fieldguide to the Birds of East Africa*. HarperCollins.

Ostrich
(Struthio cam...

The largest bird in the world standing 2 to 2.5 metres in height, and weighing up ... 130 kgs., which makes this flightless species almost impossible to misidentify. T... adult male (A) has black and white plumage, the white being restricted to the tail ... the tips of the stunted wings. The head, neck and thighs are pink. The plumage o... female (B) is a mixture of greys and browns with the head, neck and legs dull grey... brown. The Somali Ostrich (*Struthio camelus molybdophanes*, C), a sub-species, also occurs and is found in parts of Ethiopia, Somalia and Kenya. The male differ... appearance in having blue-grey neck and thighs and a red stripe on the front of th... lower leg. They prefer areas of short grass plains and dry semi-desert bush and sc... During the breeding season several females may lay in the same nest and 70+ eggs... have been recorded. It is only possible for the incubating bird, usually the 'major hen', to cover around 20 eggs so in circumstances of larger clutches many go to waste. The incubation period is 45 days and after hatching chicks from many different broods may join together into a creche. The raising and protection of the chicks, which continues for around 9 months, is often undertaken by a 'major pair... with other adults in loose association. Resident. Size 2 to 2.5 metres.

Great Crested Grebe
(Podiceps crista...

The largest grebe in Africa, found on large open areas of both fresh and alkaline water, where they feed almost exclusively on small fish. The forehead, crown and hindneck are blackish. The sides of the face, throat, foreneck and underparts are white. In breeding plumage the ear coverts become chestnut edged with black and the feathering on the crown lengthens and forms into a crest. The back is blackish streaked with brown. The bill is black with a reddish tinge. The eyes are red. The sexes are similar. Resident. Size 52 cms.

Black-necked Grebe
(Podiceps nigricol...

A small grebe of both freshwater and alkaline lakes and ponds. In breeding pluma... the head, neck and back are black contrasting with striking golden-yellow ear coverts. The flanks are chestnut and the underside almost pure white. They are oft... encountered in flocks during non-breeding periods, when the plumage on the forehead, crown, nape, hindneck, back and wings is greyish-black, the throat, foreneck and underparts are off-white. The bill is dark grey-black and curves slight... upwards. The eyes are orange-red. The sexes are alike. Resident. Size 30 cms.

Little Grebe
(Tachybaptus ruficoli...

The commonest grebe on the freshwater and alkaline lakes of the rift valley. They a... also found on small ponds and sluggish rivers. A small, squat grebe with the forehead, crown and hindneck black. The cheeks, throat and foreneck are rich chestnut, and the back and wings are brown. The flanks are rufous and the breast a... underparts white. The short bill is dark with a patch of cream at the base. The eyes are dark red. The plumage becomes duller and greyer during non-breeding periods. The sexes are alike. Resident. Size 25 cms.

White Pelican
(Pelecanus onocrota...

Recognisable when at rest or on water by their almost completely white plumage which often has a flush of pink during the breeding season. In flight the black primary and secondary wing feathers are prominent. The large bill is greyish-yell and the pouch yellow to pinkish-white. Immature birds are greyish-brown, becoming whiter with age. The legs and feet are orange-pink. The eyes are dark brown and surrounded by a patch of unfeathered pink skin. A very gregarious bir normally fishing in groups on freshwater and alkaline lakes. Resident. Size 165 cr

Pink-backed Pelican
(Pelecanus rufesc...

Found on large lakes throughout the region, usually fishing singly. Smaller and greyer in appearance than the White Pelican (*Pelecanus onocrotalus*) they have loosely arranged mottled grey feathering on the back, wings and breast, which oft gives a shaggy appearance. In flight the back and rump show a flush of pink. The primary and secondary wing feathers are blackish-brown. The bill is grey-pink an the pouch pink with streaks of yellow. The eyes are dark brown surrounded by are of bare grey-pink skin. The legs and feet are yellow. In breeding plumage they develop an eye patch of black, yellow and pink, and a crest of grey feathers on the crown. Immature birds have pale grey-brown plumage. Resident. Size 132 cms.

White-necked Cormorant
(Phalacrocorax carl...

A common waterbird of freshwater and alkaline lakes as well as rivers and, to a lesser extent, coastal regions. A large blackish-brown bird with white throat and fore-neck and, in breeding plumage, a white patch to the sides of the rump and a crest of black feathers on the crown. Immature birds are duller and browner than adults with the throat, neck, breast and belly white, streaked and flecked with greyish-brown. The bill is dark with an red-orange mark on the lores. The eyes are emerald green. They are normally found in large flocks, feeding by pursuing fish underwater and are often seen following a feeding session, perched with wings spread to dry. Resident. Size 90 cms.

Long-tailed Cormorant
(Phalacrocorax african...

Usually found singly or in small groups. A common and widespread bird of freshwater lakes, rivers and coastal areas. A much smaller cormorant than the Whit necked with almost entirely black plumage and a small crest of erectile feathers on the forehead. The wing coverts are distinctly marked with silver-grey. In breeding plumage white plume feathers appear to the rear of the eyes. The tail is long. The bi is yellow and the eyes a rich red, the legs and feet are black. Immature birds have upper-parts brown-black while the underparts are white flecked and streaked with brown. Resident. Size 58 cms.

African Darter
(Anhinga rufa...

A bird of freshwater lakes, rivers and marshes widely distributed throughout the region. Distinguished from the cormorants by the thin, pointed bill, small slender head and long thin neck. The forehead, crown, hind-neck, back and tail are black. The front and sides of the neck are chestnut edged with white. The wings are black streaked with white and the underparts are all black. The rich colours of the head and neck are less pronounced in the female. Immatures resemble females but have underparts of brown. They are solitary feeders pursuing fish underwater which the spear with their dagger-like bills. Like the cormorants they will often perch with wings out-stretched to dry following a feeding session. Resident. Size 95 cms.

Night Heron
(Nycticorax nyctico)

Primarily nocturnal this distinctive heron hides away in thick waterside vegetati
during much of the day. The crown, hind-neck, mantle and scapulars of adult bir
(A) are a glossy black, often showing a green-blue sheen. The forehead, throat, fro
and sides of the neck, breast and underparts are white. The wings and tail are gre
The legs and feet are bright yellow and the eyes are rich crimson. During the breedi
season 2 or 3 long white plumes flow from the crown. The bill is dark almost blac
The sexes are alike. Immature birds (B) have dark brown upper-parts flecked and
spotted with white, and buff-grey underparts streaked with dark-brown. Residen
numbers increase with the arrival of palearctic winter visitors. Size 60 cms.

Squacco Heron
(Ardeola rallor

Common and widely distributed throughout East Africa, frequenting lakes, rivers
streams, marshes and ponds. A small brownish-buff heron with a rich cinnamon
crown, nape and hindneck. During the breeding season long black and white
feathers appear on the crown and plumes of cinnamon feathers flow from the
mantle. The throat, neck and underparts are white. In flight the white wings, rum
and tail contrast strongly with the darker areas of plumage. The bill legs and feet a
yellowish-green. The sexes are alike. Immature birds have the crown and breast
streaked with dark brown. Resident and winter visitor from the palearctic region.
Size 45 cms.

Cattle Egret
(Bubulcus i

A very common and widely distributed bird of open plains, lakes rivers and
marshes. Often in association with plains game animals, feeding on insects
disturbed from the grasses by the grazing herds. The plumage is almost entirely
white during periods of non-breeding. At breeding times golden-buff elongated
plumes appear on the crown the breast and the mantle. The bill is yellow-orange, t
legs and feet yellow or pale orange-pink. The sexes are alike. Immatures resemble
non-breeding adults but with the bill, legs and feet black. Resident. Size 50 cms.

Green-backed Heron
(Butorides striat

Widely distributed throughout East Africa frequenting lakes, rivers, marshes,
estuaries and coastal areas. A small heron with a dark green crown and nape. The
mantle and the sides of the neck and hindneck are grey. The upper breast is rufous
and the underparts are light grey. The wings are dark green above and grey below.
The legs and feet are yellowish-green and the bill is black with a yellowish base. Th
sexes are similar, females tend to be slightly duller in appearance. Immatures are
browner, streaked and spotted with white above and dark brown below. Resident.
Size 40 cms.

Great White Egret
(Egretta alb

The largest egret to be found in East Africa. Widely distributed and quite common
on lakes and other expanses of open water both inland and coastal. The plumage is
completely white, the legs and feet are black and the bill, during the breeding seaso
is black with a variable amount of yellow towards the base. During periods of non-
breeding the bill is yellow. The eyes are red during the breeding period and yellow a
other times. The sexes are alike. Immature birds resemble non-breeding adults.
Resident. Size 90 cms.

Yellow-billed Egret
(Egretta intermedi

Widespread and reasonably common on freshwater lakes as well as in coastal areas.
Like a smaller version of the Great White Egret (*Egretta alba*), the Yellow-billed Egre
has all white plumage. The legs and feet are black and the bill is yellow-orange. The
eyes are yellow during periods of non-breeding and, like the bill, turn redder during
the breeding season. The sexes are alike. Immature birds are similar to non-breeding
adults. Resident. Size 65 cms.

Little Egret
(Egretta garz

A widely distributed species on lakes, swamps, marshes, ponds and in coastal regions. A small egret with entirely white plumage, easily identified by the black legs and bright yellow feet. The bill is grey-black and the eyes are yellow. During breeding season they develop long thin plume feathers which flow from the rear the crown and from the mantle and lower foreneck. The sexes are alike. The immatures resemble non-breeding adults. Resident and palearctic winter visitor. Size 58 cms.

Black Heron
(Egretta ardes

Although widely distributed in East Africa it is not an easy bird to locate. They frequent marshes, lakes, rivers and coastal mudflats. The plumage is slate grey-bl with plumes on the nape, mantle and lower foreneck. The legs are black and the fe yellow. The bill is grey-black and the eyes are yellow. Normally found in flocks, feeding by forming a canopy with the wings thereby shading the water surface fro reflections and attracting potential prey into the shade. The sexes are alike. Resid Size 56 cms.

Grey Heron
(Ardea cine

A common and widespread species on lakes, swamps and marshes. A large heron with body and wing plumage grey-blue. The forehead, crown, chin, face and neck are white. A black stripe extends from above and behind the eyes to the back of the crown from which flow several long black plumes. A line of black streaks extends down the centre of the foreneck terminating at the white breast. The belly, wing ti and shoulders are black, the bill, legs and feet greyish-yellow. The eyes are bright yellow. The sexes are alike. Immature birds are generally paler and duller than adults, with underparts streaked with brown. Resident and palearctic winter visite Size 100 cms.

Black-headed Heron
(Ardea melanocephe

An inhabitant of areas of permanent open water, marshes, swamps and rivers throughout East Africa. The plumage of the upper and lower body, the tail and the wings is dark slaty blue-grey. The chin and throat are white. The upper portion of t head, from just below the eyes, is black extending over the nape and hindneck merging with the slate-grey of the mantle. The lower neck is white heavily marked and streaked with black. The legs and feet are black. The bill is grey-black and the eyes bright yellow. The sexes are alike. Immature birds are browner with off-white underparts. Resident. Size 96 cms.

Goliath Heron
(Ardea goliat

The largest heron in Africa, with mainly slate-grey upper body and wing plumage. The head and neck are chestnut brown. The chin, throat and foreneck are white wit the lower part of the neck heavily streaked with black. The underparts and thighs ar deep chestnut, the legs and feet are black. The bill is grey-black and the eyes are yellow. The sexes are alike. Immatures are duller and paler than adults, showing more brown in the body and wing plumage. The underparts are lighter and streaked with browns. Resident. Size 150 cms.

Purple Heron
(Ardea purpurec

An inhabitant of lakes, swamps and marshes throughout East Africa. A slim heron readily distinguished from the Grey Heron (*Ardea cinerea*) by the bright rufous feathering of the neck and head. The plumage of the upper body and wings is slate-grey washed with rufous. The forehead and crown are black, two black stripes extend from the gape, one following a line to the nape and down the hindneck, whilst the other extends down the sides of the neck to the breast. The throat and foreneck are white heavily streaked with black. The breast, belly and shoulders are chestnut. The bill is deep yellow, the legs and feet yellow-black and the eyes yellow. The sexes are alike. Immatures are paler and mottled in appearance. Resident and palearctic winter visitor. Size 85 cms.

24

Hammerkop
(Scopus umb...

Occurs throughout the region in suitable areas usually in the vicinity of water. A... with a dull russet brown plumage paler on the cheeks, neck and breast. A large c... on the crown and nape gives the bird a distinctive hammerhead appearance. Th... substantial bill is black as are the legs and feet. The eyes are dark brown. The se... are alike. Immature birds are similar to adults. Resident. Size 60 cms.

Abdim's Stork
(Ciconia ab...

A gregarious stork with head, neck, upperparts and wings metallic purple-black... breast, belly, underparts and rump are white. The bill is yellow-green. There are... patches of unfeathered skin on the face, red in front of the eyes and blue on the c... The legs and feet are greenish with a flush of red around the joints. The eyes are... brown. The sexes are similar. Immatures have a browner appearance with facial... patches, bill and legs duller. Small numbers do breed in East Africa but the vast... majority are migrants. Size 80 cms.

Black Stork
(Ciconia n...

This species can be confused with Abdim's Stork (*Ciconia abdimii*) but differs in... being larger and having the bill, legs and feet red. The upperparts, tail, breast and... wings are glossy black with a green-purple metallic sheen. The lower breast, bell... and underparts are white. The eyes are dark brown surrounded by a red area of... unfeathered skin. The sexes are alike. Immatures lack the red facial patch which... appears grey and have the bill, legs and feet greyish-green. A migrant visitor to Ea... Africa. Size 96 cms.

White Stork
(Ciconia cico...

Often found in large flocks feeding on grasshoppers and other insects on the ope... savannahs. The head, neck, back, breast, wing coverts and underparts are white, ... primary wing feathers black. The large bill, long, thin legs and feet are red. The ey... are dark brown. The sexes are alike. Immatures have primary feathers tinged with... brown and brown-red bill, legs and feet. A palearctic winter migrant. Size 102 cm...

Woolly-necked Stork
(Ciconia episco...

An inhabitant of lakes, rivers and coastal areas over much of East Africa, usually... found singly. The upperparts, wings and breast are glossy blue-black. The head is... white with a black crown, the neck is white and has a woolly appearance. The bel... and underparts are white. The bill is blackish, red towards the tip, the legs and fee... are blackish and the eyes are blood red. The sexes are alike. Immature birds lack t... white forehead and have browner upperparts and wings. Resident. Size 85 cms.

Saddle-billed Stork
(Ephippiorhynchus senegalen...

East Africa's largest stork. The head, neck, tail and wing coverts are black. The bac... breast, belly and underparts are white as are the primary and secondary wing... feathers. The bill is large and has a slightly upturned appearance, the base and tip... bright red and the broad centre section is black. On top of the bill in front of the... forehead, sits a bright yellow saddle. The extremely long legs are black with the fee... and joints red. The sexes are similar, the female is smaller and has a bright yellow... eye, the eye is dark brown in the male. Immatures are dull, rather grey birds lackin... the bright features of the adults. Resident. Size 168 cms.

Openbill Stork
(Anastomus lamellig

A gregarious stork of lakes, rivers, swamps and marshes over much of East Africa
The plumage is entirely glossy black-brown often showing an iridescent sheen o
bronze-green. The bill is yellow-brown becoming whitish towards the base, the
shape is unique among storks in that the upper and lower mandibles meet only a
base and tip, having a prominent gap towards the centre. This specialised bill all
the bird to feed on freshwater mussels and snails, prising open the hard exterior
shells with ease. The legs and feet are blackish. The sexes are alike. Immatures ar
duller and browner, particularly the underparts, and have white flecking on the
hindneck. The bill is also less well developed, the gap gradually widening with a
Resident. Size 90 cms.

Marabou Stork
(Leptoptilos crumenif

An extremely large and widely distributed stork with a rather grotesque appearance.
The upperparts, wings and tail are blue-black. The breast, belly and underparts are
white. The head is unfeathered, pink to red in colour and mottled with black at the b
of the bill, the forehead and around the eyes. The neck is white and sparsely feathere
but has a ruff of whitish feathers at the base. The bill is pale yellow-cream. The legs a
feet are grey-black, but quite often 'whitened' with droppings. A large pendulous pin
throat pouch is often present. The sexes are alike. Resident. Size 150 cms.

Yellow-billed Stork
(Mycteria

Widespread and very common in suitable habitats, lakes, marshes and swamps
being favoured. The head, neck, upper and underparts, back, breast and belly are
white, often with a flush of pink. The tail and primary wing feathers are black. Th
face and forehead are bright red and the long bill is bright yellow. The legs and fee
are bright red. The eyes are dark brown. The sexes are alike. Immature birds are
duller with the body feathering light to mid-grey. Resident. Size 105 cms.

Sacred Ibis
(Threskiornis aethiopi

Widely distributed throughout East Africa, usually in wet habitats but often in are
of cultivated land. The body plumage is white, the wings have black tips to the
primary feathers. Long black plumes flow from the lower back over the tail. The
head and neck are black and unfeathered. The black bill is long and decurved. The
legs and feet are black. Patches of bare skin on the underwing show bright red in
flight. The eyes are dark brown. The sexes are alike. Resident. Size 75 cms.

Hadada Ibis
(Bostrychia hageda

An inhabitant of wooded river sides and open forests. The upperparts and wings a
bronze-grey with an iridescent sheen of green particularly on the wings. The head,
neck, breast and belly are grey-brown and a white stripe extends from the gape
across the lower cheek. The long decurved bill is black with a red stripe along the t
of the upper mandible. The legs and feet are grey-black with the tops of the toes
striped red. The eyes are pale yellow. The sexes are alike. Immatures are a dull
version of the adults. Resident. Size 75 cms.

Glossy Ibis
(Plegadis falcinell

Under certain lighting conditions the Glossy Ibis appears entirely black, although i
actual fact the plumage is brown with an array of iridescent greens and purples. Th
head and neck are lightly flecked with white. The long decurved bill is a dull dark
flesh pink. The legs and feet are greenish-brown often darkening at the joints. The
eyes are dark brown. The sexes are alike. Immature birds are generally browner tha
adults. Resident and palearctic winter visitor. Size 60 cms.

African Spoonbill
(Platalea ...

Occurs over much of East Africa favouring both fresh and alkaline lakes, rivers, marshes and swamps. A bird with pure white plumage. The forehead, front of face and chin are bright red and unfeathered. The most obvious identification feature the large spoon-like pink and grey bill which is used in a sweeping motion when feeding. The legs and feet are pink-red. The sexes are alike. Immatures have plum streaked with brown and lack strong colour in the face, bill and legs, the feet are black. Resident. Size 90 cms.

Greater Flamingo
(Phoenicopterus ru...

The larger of East Africa's flamingoes they occur in large numbers throughout the valley, frequenting alkaline and freshwater lakes. The head, long slender neck, ba underparts and tail are white with a flush of pink. The wing coverts are bright sca and the primary and secondary wing feathers are black. The bill is broad and curv bright pink with a black tip. It is specially adapted for filtering small prey items fr shallow water. The long thin legs and feet are vivid pink. The sexes are similar, th female being smaller. Immatures are brown-grey in plumage with grey-black bill a legs. Resident. Size 140 cms.

Lesser Flamingo
(Phoenicopterus mi...

Found in enormous flocks on the alkaline lakes of the rift valley. The plumage var from almost pure white, in young and non-breeding birds, to pale rose pink during breeding periods. The primary wing feathers are black and the wing coverts deep crimson. The bill is broad and curved, black at the base and the tip with a varying amount of deep red in the centre portion. The eyes are bright yellow-orange and th long, thin legs and feet are bright red. The female is smaller and paler in colour tha the male. Immature birds have a grey-brown plumage. Resident. Size 100 cms.

Fulvous Whistling Duck
(Dendrocygna bico...

A duck of freshwater lakes, rivers and flood plains throughout East Africa. An upstanding, erect duck with rufous plumage, generally darker brown on the hindneck, back and scapulars. The rump and tail are black, The upper tail cover are white and prominent in flight. Some white flecking occurs on the upper flan The foreneck and throat are buff darkening to rufous-brown on the lower breast and belly. The undertail coverts are white. The bill and long legs are blue-grey. T sexes are alike. Immature birds resemble adults but have paler plumage. Residen Size 50 cms.

White-faced Tree Duck
(Dendrocygna vidua...

A very gregarious and distinctive duck inhabiting inland lakes, swamps and marshes. An upright, long-necked duck with the frontal portion of the head, face an throat white, the rear of the head and upper neck are black and the remainder of the neck and breast is chestnut. The belly and underparts are black and the flanks and sides of the breast are white, boldly barred with black. The mantle and wing covert are olive-brown and the rump and tail black. The bill is black with a blue band towards the tip. The legs and feet are bluish and the eyes dark brown. The sexes are alike. Resident. Size 46 cms.

Egyptian Goose
(Alopochen aegyptiac...

A common and widely distributed goose, favouring inland waters, swamps and rivers. Predominantly grey-buff on the head, fore-neck, breast, belly, back, underparts and flanks. A dark brown patch encircles the orange eyes. The nape and wing coverts are chestnut and an irregular blotch of chestnut feathers can be seen or the lower breast. The rump, tail and primary wing feathers are black. The secondary wing feathers have an iridescent sheen of metallic green. The bill is dark pink and the legs and feet a rich red. The sexes are similar, the females being slightly smaller. Resident. Size 60 cms.

Spur-winged Goose
(Plectropterus gambens

The largest goose in Africa, found in aquatic habitats, grasslands and areas of cultivated crops. The upperbody, neck, back of head and wings are bronze-black with the latter often showing a sheen of iridescent green. The underparts from the lower breast to the tail coverts are white. The face is white to the rear of the eyes and pink-red to the fore. The bill, which often has a knob at the base of the upper mandible, is deep red with a pale tip. The legs and feet are pinkish-red. The female is duller and smaller than the male. Immatures are browner and lack the bright bare pink-red facial patch. Resident. Size 84 cms.

Knob-billed Duck
(Sarkidiornis melonoto

A substantial black and white duck of lakes and rivers throughout the region. The upperparts and wings are blackish with washes of iridescent greens and purples. The rump is brown. The head and neck are white speckled with black. The breast, belly and undertail coverts are white and the flanks grey. The bill is black, the males having a large swelling at the base of the upper mandible during the breeding season. The legs and feet are grey-black. Females are smaller less well marked and lack the knob on the bill. Resident. Size 60 cms.

Cape Teal
(Anas capensis

A small duck encountered mainly on alkaline lakes and shallow pools over much of the region. The back and scapulars are dark brown edged with buff. The breast and underparts are grey-white as are the flanks which are blotched with brown. The head and neck are grey finely speckled with brown. The bill is pink with a black base, the legs and feet are grey-yellow. The eyes are orange-brown. The sexes are alike. Immature birds resemble adults but lack strong bill and eye colour. Resident. Size 35 cms.

Wigeon
(Anas penelope,

A palearctic winter visitor which can be found on freshwater lakes and coastal mudflats, often in large flocks. The males have a cinnamon red head and neck, with a patch of light buff on the forehead and crown. The breast, belly, flanks and mantle are greyish-white. The tail coverts are black and the primary wing feathers brown-black. The bill is slate-grey with a black tip, the legs and feet are grey. The female has a mottled plumage of buff, grey and reddish-browns. Some non-breeding individuals remain year round but the vast majority are migratory. Size 45 cms.

Yellow-billed Duck
(Anas undulata)

Distributed over much of the region being very abundant in some areas. Found on freshwater lakes and marshes. Most of the body feathering is dark brown with buff-white edging, the underparts and tail are dark brown. The head and neck are brown with fine buff streaking. The wings, in certain lights, show a flash of iridescent green. The eyes are brown and the bill bright yellow with a patch of black around the base and the tip. The legs and feet are brown-black. The female is smaller and generally less bright. Resident. Size 50 cms.

Red-billed Duck
(Anas erythrorhynchos)

A common and widely distributed species in suitable habitats. Present on freshwater lakes, marshes and flood plains. The feathers on the upperparts and scapulars are dark brown edged with buff. The breast, belly and flanks are buff-white with brown crescent speckling darkest on the flanks. The top of the head, from the base of the bill to the nape and the hindneck, is dark brown-black, the rest of the head and face being buff-white. The bill is bright red, the eyes dark brown and the legs and feet blue-grey. The sexes are alike. Resident. Size 38 cms.

Garganey Teal
(Anas querquedula)

A palearctic winter migrant to freshwater lakes and flood plains. The most distinctive field marking of the male garganey is the broad white stripe extending from the side of the forehead through the eye to the nape and hindneck, contrasting with the dark brown head. The breast is brown marked with black crescent barring. The belly and underparts are white finely barred with black. The wing coverts and scapulars are dark bluish-green the latter edged with white. The primary wing feathers are brown. The bill is dark and the legs and feet dark blue-grey. Females have browner underparts with much blotching and streaking. The head is dark brown with buff eyebrow and cheek stripes above and below a dark eye stripe. The underparts are white. A palearctic winter visitor. Size 38 cms.

Shoveler
(Anas clypeata)

Easily recognised by the large dark grey-black spatulate bill, with which it dabbles for food in it's favoured habitat of shallow freshwater lakes and marshes. The head is glossy bottle green, the breast white and the belly and flanks chestnut. The back and rump are grey-black, the scapulars are dull green, black and white. The eyes are bright yellow, the legs and feet orange-red. The female is generally brown with buff feather edges, the bill and eye colour is much reduced. A palearctic winter visitor. Size 50 cms.

Hottentot Teal
(Anas hottentota)

The smallest duck in East Africa, favouring shallow lakes, ponds and marshes fringed with reeds. Males have a dark brown-black forehead, crown and nape, contrasting with a buff-white face. A blackish patch is present to the rear of the head adjacent to the nape. The breast and underparts are tawny-white spotted and barred with dark brown and black. The back, rump and tail are brown-black. The wing feathering is mostly dark brown edged with buff, the secondaries showing a greenish iridescent gloss. The bill, legs and feet are slate blue-grey. The eyes are dark brown. Females are generally duller and lack barring on the underparts. Resident. Size 28 cms.

Maccoa Duck
(Oxyura maccoa)

A stiff-tailed diving duck of shallow open waters fringed with tall, dense emergent vegetation. The males have the head and upper neck black with the breast, mantle, flanks and tail coverts a bright chestnut. The underparts are grey-brown and the tail feathers are black and often held stiffly at an angle of about 45 degrees. The bill is bright blue, the eyes dark brown and the legs and feet dull grey. The females and non-breeding males have grey-brown upperparts flecked with buff, light brown flanks with fine buff-white flecking. The head has a grey-brown cap below which is a whitish stripe extending from the base of the upper mandible towards the nape. The chin, throat and lower neck are whitish. Resident. Size 44 cms.

Secretary Bird
(Sagittarius serpentarius)

Almost unmistakable. A large long-legged bird of prey usually encountered in pairs walking across the open short grass savannahs in search of snakes, lizards, small rodents and large invertebrates on which they feed. The forehead, crown, nape, mantle and wing coverts are light grey and the chin, neck and throat are off-white. Long flowing, black tipped crest feathers emerge from the nape. A patch of unfeathered skin surrounds the eyes and varies in colour from yellow-orange to bright red. The belly, thighs and wing feathers are black. The grey tail is very long with the central feathers banded black at the tip. The eyes are brown and the legs and feet pale pink. The bill is grey with a flush of yellow at the base. Resident. Size 100 cms.

Ruppell's Griffon Vulture
(Gyps ruppell..

A large common vulture of savannah and hill regions in the vicinity of gorges and cliffs which are required for roosting and nesting. The head and neck are covered with sparse downy grey-white feathers, often becoming dirty, matted and soiled when feeding. They have a fluffy white ruff at the base of the neck. The back, wing coverts and speculars are dark brown edged with white, the primary feathers are dark brown-black. The feathering of the underparts is brown with buff-cream edges and tips. The bill is cream, the legs and feet are dull grey-brown. The sexes are alike Immature birds lack white feathering on the head and neck and the pale feather edges are less well defined. With young birds taking at least seven years to attain full adult plumage the variation is extreme and varied. Resident. Size 86 cms.

White-backed Vulture
(Gyps africanu..

The commonest and most widespread of East Africa's vultures. The head and neck are black, sparsely covered with downy grey-white feathers. The off-white neck ruff is rather thinly feathered. The mantle is dark brown, the wing coverts sandy brown and the primary wing feathers and tail are brown-black. The back and rump are white, very pronounced in flight. The bill, legs and feet are black. The sexes are alike. Immature birds are darker than the adults, taking six to seven years to attain full adult plumage. This results in many plumage variations. Resident. Size 80 cms.

Nubian Vulture
(Aegypius tracheliotus,

The largest vulture in Africa, inhabiting open grassland savannahs. The unfeathered head and neck are pink to red, with flaps and folds of skin on the sides of the head and crown. At the base of the neck is a short, spiky ruff of dark brown feathers. The upperparts and wings are dark brown-black. The flanks, thighs and underparts are covered with white, downy feathers. The breast has long brown feathers edged with white. The eyes are dark brown. The massive bill is dark grey-blue tipped with dull yellow. The legs and feet are grey-blue. The sexes are similar, the female being slightly larger than the male. Immature birds are browner in plumage with the head and neck paler. Resident. Size 100 cms.

White-headed Vulture
(Aegypius occipitalis)

Distinct among East Africa's vultures in having a pronounced white-pink head. A collar of dark brown-black feathers sits around the neck. The back, tail and wing coverts are brown-black, the secondaries are white and the primaries black. The belly, thighs and undertail coverts are white. The bill is red towards the tip and pale blue at the base. The legs and feet are pink. The sexes are alike. Generally seen less often than other vulture species. Resident. Size 80 cms.

Hooded Vulture
(Necrosyrtes monachus)

A widespread and common species in savannah and grassland areas. A small vulture with head and neck pinkish-red. The body plumage is almost entirely mid-brown with darker brown-black tail and wing feathers. A 'hood' of tight pale grey feathering covers the hindneck, nape and crown. The thin bill is light grey-pink at the base darkening towards the tip. The legs and feet are light grey-blue. The sexes are alike. Immature birds have face and neck white and the 'hood' brown. Resident. Size 70 cms.

Egyptian Vulture
(Neophron Percnopterus)

A widespread but sparsely scattered species frequenting savannah and open plains. A small vulture with plumage almost entirely white, the exceptions being the black secondary and primary wing feathers. The unfeathered area of the face is bright yellow-orange. The feathering on the crown, nape and throat has a shaggy appearance. The legs and feet are pale yellow-pink. The dark brown bill is long and thin. The sexes are alike with the female slightly larger. Immature birds are generally browner and quite easily confused with the hooded vulture which has a rounded tail unlike the longer wedge-shaped tail of the Egyptian. Resident. Size 68 cms.

Palm Nut Vulture

(Gypohierax angol...)

A bird of coastal forests and savannah woodlands, feeding on oil palms and asso... fruits as well as fish and amphibians. Will feed on meat occasionally, comes regularly to the leopard bait put out at Samburu Lodge in northern Kenya. The he... neck, breast, belly and wing coverts are white. The scapulars and secondaries ar... black and the primary wing feathers white tipped with black. The tail is black an... has a white tip. The orange-yellow eyes are surrounded by patches of bright oran... red unfeathered skin, a similar patch is present on the chin. The legs and feet are flesh pink. The sexes are alike. Resident. Size 70 cms.

African Marsh Harrier

(Circus ranive...)

Inhabits a wide range of habitats from open grasslands, lake edges, swamps and marshes to cultivated fields of wheat. The plumage is mainly dark brown streake... and blotched with rufous. The throat, breast and belly are white streaked with browns. The upper tail is brown banded with brown-black, lighter below barred with grey. The plumage variation is considerable. The eyes are yellow. The sexes ... similar. They usually hunt by slowly flying at ten to fifty feet above the ground, fr... where they pursue small birds or pounce on small mammals, reptile, amphibians... and insects. Resident. Size 50 cms.

Montagu's Harrier

(Circus pygar...)

A palearctic winter visitor during which times they become the commonest harrie... of open grassland areas. Feeding on small birds and mammals, reptiles, amphibia... and large insects. The males have upperbody plumage of pale blue-grey. The throa... and breast are grey and the undertail coverts white. The underwings and flanks ar... white, heavily barred with chestnut, the upperwing has a distinctive black wing b... along the secondaries, the primaries are black. The eyes, legs and feet are bright yellow. The female is dark brown on the upper wing surfaces, the under wings are buff streaked and barred with browns. The tail is dark brown heavily banded with blackish-brown. The rump is white. The throat, breast and belly are buff streaked and flecked with rufous. Winter visitor. Size 45 cms.

Pallid Harrier

(Circus macrour...)

A palearctic winter visitor inhabiting open grasslands where they hunt small birds and mammals, grasshoppers, locusts and other large insects. At a distance the mal... may be confused with Montagu's Harrier (*Circus pygargus*) but is generally paler ar... lacks the black wing bar and the rufous barring on the flanks and underwings. The female is very similar to the female Montagu's Harrier but lacks the chestnut underwing barring, this is however very difficult to observe unless very close view... are obtained. The eyes, legs and feet are yellow. Winter visitor. Size 48 cms.

Harrier Hawk

(Polyboroides typ...)

An inhabitant of forests and woodlands. The face is unfeathered and bright yellow-pink. The head, neck, mantle and breast are slate blue-grey. The lower breast, flank... thighs and underparts are white with heavy black barring. The wing coverts and scapulars are grey with black blotches. The primary wing feathers are black. The tai... is long and broad, black with white bands across the centre, the base and the tip. Th... legs are yellow and very long aiding the bird to extract young from the nests of othe... birds, particularly tree hole and tunnel nesters. They also feed on fruits, small mammals, reptiles and insects. The sexes are similar, the female being larger and more heavily barred. Resident. Size 68 cms.

Bateleur Eagle
(Terathopius ecau

One of the easiest eagles to identify in flight, having an extremely short tail and broad wings. The adult male (A) has the head, neck, breast and belly black. The tail and feathers of the mantle are chestnut, although a light phase does occur in which the mantle is grey-cream. The wing coverts are pale brown-white. The up surface of the primary and secondary wing feathers are black, the underside wh with black tips to the primaries. On the face there is a patch of bright red unfeath skin at the base of the bill, the cere is bright red and the bill orange-red with a da tip. The eyes are brown and the legs and feet red with dark talons. The female is slightly larger than the male and has secondary wing feathers grey-brown. In flig only a narrow band of black is visible along the trailing edge of the wings, this is much broader in the male. Immature birds (B) are pale brown with variable amo of streaking and flecking. The unfeathered facial patch and the cere are pale blue green, the bill, legs and feet pale grey. It takes up to seven years for immatures to attain full adult plumage. Resident. Size 60 cms.

Black-chested Harrier Eagle
(Circaetus pecto

Sparsely distributed over much of the region, favouring areas of lightly wooded savannah and thin woodlands. The head, neck, throat, breast and back are dark brown-black. The wings are dark brown with some feathers edged with pale buff-white. The belly and thighs are pure white. The eyes are a very bright yellow contrasting strongly with the dark plumage of the face and head. The bill is dull blue-grey and the legs and feet flesh pink-grey. The sexes are similar, the female being slightly larger than the male. There is much variation in the plumage of immature birds which are dark brown above and pale rufous brown below. They often to be seen perched in the high branches of trees from where they scan the ground below for snakes, lizards and amphibians, occasionally also taking birds a small mammals. Resident. Size 70 cms.

Shikra
(Accipiter bad

Found throughout lowland areas of East Africa in woodlands and lightly wooded savannahs with tall rank grass undergrowth. They feed on small birds and mamm lizards, amphibians and insects. The adult male has the head, back, wings and tai plain slate grey. The face, throat, breast, belly and underparts are whitish with a flush of pink. The lower breast, belly, flanks and thighs are barred with rufous brown. The eyes are yellow-orange. The legs and feet are yellow-pink, the cere is yellow and the bill blue-grey. The female is larger than the male, darker grey above and with bolder barring below and on the flanks. Resident. Size 30 cms.

Little Sparrowhawk
(Accipiter minull

Found over much of the region but seldom seen as a result of spending much of the time in dense woodlands and thickets, where they hunt small birds and insects. Th adult male has head, neck, back and wings dark slate-grey. The upper tail is black with two ragged white stripes across the centre, below the tail is grey-white with bold banding. The breast, belly flanks and underparts are white barred with rufous brown. The throat and rump are pure white, the latter being very pronounced in flight. The eyes, cere, legs and feet are yellow. The bill is dark. The female is brown above and more heavily barred below. Immature birds are dark brown above, streaked with buff, the underside is white boldly marked with irregular blotches of dark brown. Resident. Size 28 cms.

Pale Chanting Goshawk

(Melierax ca...)

A long-legged bird of prey with an upright posture. Found over much of the regi... where it favours areas of dry bush and sparse woodlands. Adult birds (B) have h... neck, mantle, back and wing coverts pale slaty grey. The primary wing feathers ... black edged with grey. The chin, throat and upper breast are pale grey. The lowe... breast, belly, thighs and flanks are white finely barred with dark grey. The rump... pure white and very prominent when seen in flight. The tail is white below whi... above the centre feathers are black with the outer feathers barred grey and white... cere is orange-yellow and the tip of the bill is dark. The long legs and feet are red... The eyes are dark brown. The sexes are similar. Immature birds (A) are dull grey... brown on the head, nape, back and wing coverts. The primaries are black, the secondaries grey-brown edged with black. The belly, thighs and flanks are grey-white barred with brown. The throat and breast are grey-white heavily streaked brown. The cere and bill are grey-blue. The eyes, legs and feet are pale yellow. O... seen in the early morning hunting from favoured perches. They feed on lizards, insects, small mammals and birds ranging from small passerines to francolins. W... often spend time walking in areas of open ground in search of reptiles and insect... Resident. Size 48 cms.

Dark Chanting Goshawk

(Melierax metab...)

Inhabits open acacia woodland and thornbush country, usually in the west of the region. The head, neck, mantle, back and wing coverts are dark slate grey. The primary wing feathers are black edged with grey. The throat and upper breast are grey, the lower breast, belly, flanks and underparts are grey-white finely barred w... dark grey. Very similar in posture and appearance to pale chanting goshawk but t... upperparts are a darker grey, the rump is white barred with grey and the cere is bright red. Immature birds are dark brown above, paler brown-grey below with br... streaking on the breast. Usually feeds from elevated perches swooping on lizards small snakes and rodents. Will also take insects and birds up to the size of guineafowl. Resident. Size 48 cms.

Gabar Goshawk

(Micronisus ga...)

Widespread throughout East Africa in areas of woodland, particularly light thornbush. Feeds on other bird species by pursuing them in flight and by robbing nests containing young chicks. They will also take insects and lizards. Adult bird... have the head, neck, back, upper breast and wing coverts slate-grey. The rump is white, the tail grey-brown above, off-white below with four cross-bands of dark gr... black. The lower breast, belly, flanks, thighs and underwings are white barred wit... grey-brown. The cere is yellow and the bill dull blue-grey. The eyes are dark red, t... legs and feet orange-red. A melanistic phase occurs in which the entire plumage o... the upper body is black with the tail barred grey-brown and black. The sexes are similar, the female is larger than the male. Immature birds are brown above heavil... streaked on the crown. The underside is white with the throat and upper breast heavily streaked with brown. The lower breast, belly and the thighs are barred wit... brown. The tail is banded grey and brown. The eyes, legs and feet are yellow. Resident. Size 38 cms.

Augar Buzzard

(Buteo rufofusc...)

Well distributed over much of the region. Found on moorlands, in mountainous areas and hill country. The head, neck, mantle, back and wing coverts are black irregularly flecked with white. The throat, breast and underparts are white, the throat often spotted with black. The primary and secondary wing feathers are blac... barred with white. The tail is a bright chestnut offering an easy guide to identification, particularly in flight. The cere is yellow and the bill dark. The legs and feet are yellow with black talons. The sexes are similar. A melanistic phase occurs, the yellow legs contrasting strongly with the all black plumage, it does however retain the chestnut tail. They feed on a wide variety of birds, mammals, insects and reptiles including many venomous snakes. They often perch along roadside verges where they scavenge on creatures killed by passing traffic. Residen... Size 56 cms.

Long-crested Eagle
(Lophaetus occipit

A bird of forest edges and woodlands of all types throughout East Africa. Easily recognised by the long loosely feathered crest and dark brown-black plumage wh covers the entire bird with the exception of whitish feathering on the thighs, on th underwing coverts and the wing edges at the shoulders. The tail is brown-black w three broad grey bands. The eyes are golden yellow, the cere, legs and feet are yell They feed mainly on rodents, lizards and large insects. The sexes are similar, the female being slightly larger than the male. Resident. Size 55 cms.

Crowned Eagle
(Stephanoaetus corona

The largest of Africa's eagles, frequenting areas of highland forest and woodlands throughout the region. The male has the forehead and crown dark brown with cres feathers tipped with black. The remainder of the head and neck is pale to mid-brown. The chin and throat are dark brown. The breast, belly, thighs, legs and underparts are buff-white heavily barred and blotched with dark brown and black. The back and wing coverts are charcoal grey-black, the primary and secondary flig feathers are brown, barred and tipped with black. The long tail is charcoal black broadly barred with grey. The eyes are yellow. The bill is blackish with the gape an cere yellow. The large powerful feet are dull yellow. The female is larger than the male, has a shorter crest, a longer tail and is usually more heavily barred on the underside. Immature birds have the head and underparts white, with a hint of brow on the breast and black spotting on the lower flanks, thighs and legs. Resident. Size 92 cms.

Martial Eagle
(Polemaetus bellicosi

A very large eagle, widespread throughout East Africa frequenting riverine forests, dry bush and lightly wooded savannahs. The head, neck, back, wings and upper breast are dark brownish grey-black. The lower breast, belly, thighs and underparts are white conspicuously spotted dark brown-black. The tail is brown-black barred with grey-black. The eyes are bright golden yellow, the cere and feet dull yellow-green. The sexes are similar, the female being slightly larger and with bolder spottin on the breast. Immature birds are generally paler, have a white throat and lack the spotting on the underside. Resident. Size 86 cms.

Tawny Eagle
(Aquila rapax

The commonest eagle of the region. The plumage is subject to tremendous variation and can be anything from light buff to dark brown. The primary wing feathers are usually dark brown. The eyes are pale tawny-yellow. The bill is grey tipped with black and the cere is yellow as are the feet. The sexes are similar, the females being larger and often darker than the males. Resident. Size 75 cms.

Verreaux's Eagle
(Aquila verreauxii

Found in small numbers throughout the region in the vicinity of rocky outcrops and inland cliffs. The only eagle in the region almost entirely black both above and below. A white 'V' shaped line extends from shoulder to shoulder across the upper back and the base of the primary wing feathers on the underside are greyish. The eyes are dark brown with a yellow eyebrow. The cere and feet are yellow. The sexes are similar. They feed almost exclusively on rock hyrax in areas where hyrax densities are high, but will also take dik dik and young klipspringer as well as the occasional bird. Resident. Size 80 cms.

Wahlberg's Eagle
(Aquila wahlbergi

A small, slender eagle of woodlands, riverine forests, wooded savannahs and bush over much of the region. A bird of uniform brown plumage with a variable amount of streaking and flecking. Usually paler on the head, wing coverts and underparts. The tail is long, dark brown with sporadic banding. The eyes are mid brown, the cere and feet pale yellow-grey. The sexes are similar, the female being slightly larger than the male. At a distance it could well be mistaken for a tawny eagle, but the narrow wings, long tail and smaller size aid identification. Feeds on a variety of birds, mammals, reptiles and amphibians. Resident. Size 56 cms.

African Fish Eagle
(Haliaetus voc

Widely distributed in the vicinity of both alkaline and freshwater lakes, swamps, marshes and rivers. Adult birds (A) are unmistakeable having pure white head, ne mantle and breast feathers contrasting with rufous brown underparts and dark brown back and wings. The primary wing feathers are blackish. The tail is pure white. A patch of unfeathered skin in front of the eye along with the cere is bright yellow, the bill is grey-blue tipped black. The eyes are dark brown and the legs an feet yellow. The female (B) is larger than the male. Immature birds have crown an upperparts brown, cheeks and neck white, breast and underparts buff to brown heavily streaked with black. The tail is off-white with a brown terminal band. The immature plumage stages are subject to extreme variation. The cere, legs and feet lack the intense colour of the adults, being dull grey-yellow. Feeds mainly on fish but will also take some waterbirds including flamingos. Resident. Size 75 cms.

Black Kite
(Milvus migra

A very widely distributed species throughout East Africa, found in a wide variety habitats from woodlands to open plains as well as towns and cities where they scavenge on human refuse. The head, neck, mantle, back, wing coverts, and underparts are mid-brown streaked and flecked with dark brown. The tail is dark brown at the base and paler towards the deeply forked tip. The underside of the wings are rufous brown streaked and flecked with dark browns. The eyes are dark brown, the cere and gape, like the legs and feet are bright yellow. The bill is yellow darkening towards the tip. The sexes are similar, the female being slightly larger tha the male. Immature birds are generally paler above, browner below with white streaking and flecking. Resident. Size 58 cms.

Black-shouldered Kite
(Elanus caerulet

A small grey kite common over the whole region, ranging over a variety of habitats including open plains, woodlands, forests and farmland. The head, face, neck, breast, belly and underparts are white, the head, nape and breast having a blue-grey wash. The back and upper wing coverts are slate blue-grey, the median wing covert are black and very prominent in flight. The primary and secondary wing feathers ar blackish. The underwing coverts are white. The tail is white with some grey on the central feathers. The eyes are a piercing bright red contrasting strongly with the white face and dark eyebrow. The cere, legs and feet are bright yellow. The sexes are similar. They hunt from perches and by hovering, dropping onto prey which consists almost entirely of rodents. Resident. Size 33 cms.

Osprey
(Pandion haliaetu:

A winter visitor to much of the region ,frequenting large lakes, rivers and estuaries The crown and nape are white streaked with brown. A dark brown eye stripe extends from the eye down the sides of the neck to the mantle. The mantle, back and upper wing surfaces are dark brown. The throat and breast are white, the latter flecked with a variable amount of brown. The belly, thighs and underparts are white. The underwings are white with brown flecking. The upper tail is dark brown the underside is whitish with dark barring. The eyes are pale golden yellow The cere, legs and feet are pale slate grey. The sexes are similar. Feeds entirely on fish which are plucked from close to the surface of the water but on occasions will splash dive feet first, snatching fish from up to a metre below the surface. Winter visitor. Size 58 cms.

Pygmy Falcon
(Polioheirax semitorqaurtus,

A very small falcon of dry thornbush regions. Can be easily overlooked, resembling a shrike from a distance. The crown, back and wing coverts are grey-blue. The rump, face and underparts are white. The primary wing feathers and the tail are black, the latter with grey banding. The eyes are dark brown, the cere is red and the bill pale blue-grey at the base darkening towards the tip. The legs and feet are orange-red. The sexes differ in plumage, the mantle and back of the male being grey-blue while in the female they are rich chestnut brown. They feed mainly on large insects, small birds, rodents and lizards. Resident. Size 20 cms.

Lanner Falcon
(Falco biarmi

Found in a wide range of habitats from dry semi-deserts to woodland and forest edges and open country. The crown is rufous brown, the cheeks and throat white. black moustachial stripe is present, as is a black stripe from the eye to the lower nape. The upperparts are grey-brown with darker barring and streaking, the prima and secondary wing feathers are dark brown. The breast and underparts are white washed with pink, some brown blotching is visible on the flanks and thighs. The t is brown with grey banding. The dark brown eyes have a yellow orbital ring. The cere, legs and feet are yellow. The female is larger than the male and has more pronounced blotching and barring on the underside. Resident. Size 46 cms.

Peregrine Falcon
(Falcon peregrin

A strong powerfully built falcon. The crown, nape, cheeks and moustachial stripe are blackish, the back blue-grey. The chin, throat, breast and underparts are white washed with buff and boldly spotted and barred with black. The eyes are dark brown, the cere, legs and feet yellow. The female is larger than the male, browner above and with heavier spotting and barring on the underside. Occurs in a variety habitats from bush country to lakes and farmland. Resident and palearctic winter visitor. Size 46 cms.

Grey Kestrel
(Falcon ardosiace

Often found in lightly wooded areas, along side water courses and marshes, perched in a tree where they hunt mainly lizards, small rodents and some birds. The plumage is almost entirely soft slate grey, the primary wing feathers ar blackish. The cere, orbital ring, legs and feet are bright yellow. The eyes are dark brown. the sexes are similar, the female being slightly larger than the male. Resident. Size 36 cms.

Kestrel
(Falcon tinnuncul

Found over much of the region in a variety of habitats with light woodlands, as well as towns and cities. The male has crown, nape, moustachial stripe and tail slate blu grey. The mantle, back and wing coverts are pale chestnut spotted with black, the primary wing feathers are blackish-grey. The throat and belly are white-buff, the breast and flanks are buff heavily streaked and spotted with dark brown. The eyes are dark brown. The orbital ring, cere, legs and feet are yellow. The female, who is larger than the male, has the crown and nape light chestnut streaked with black and the tail pale chestnut banded with black. Resident and palearctic winter visitor. Size 35 cms.

Lesser Kestrel
(Falcon naumann

A very abundant palearctic winter visitor throughout the region. Often encountered in sizeable flocks, the male has the head, nape and tail light blue-grey, the end of the tail is black with a fine white tip. The mantle, back and wing coverts are plain light chestnut. The primary wing feathers are blackish. The chin, throat, breast, flanks and underparts are creamy-white with loose black spotting on the breast and flanks. The eyes are dark brown. The orbital ring, cere, legs and feet are yellow. The female has the crown and nape pale chestnut streaked with black. The tail is pale chestnut with numerous black bands. The chestnut back and wing coverts are streaked and flecked with dark brown. Palearctic winter visitor. Size 30 cms.

Greater Kestrel
(Falcon rupilocoides

Distribution restricted to western Kenya, northern Tanzania and eastern Uganda. Can be easily mistaken for a female kestrel (*Falcon tinnunculus*) but has plumage more straw colour than chestnut, blackish barring on the rump, tail, mantle and flanks and eyes of creamy-white. The sexes are alike. Immatures have barred rump and a rufous not grey tail, dark brown eyes, and cere and orbital ring blue-green. Resident. Size 36 cms.

Coqui Francolin
(Francolinus co...

Found in Tanzania, central Kenya and southern Uganda, an inhabitant of open grasslands and lightly wooded savannahs. The male has the crown and nape rich rufous brown blotched with grey-black. The face and neck are ochre yellow, the mantle and breast are white with distinctive black barring. The back and wings are mosaic of chestnut, grey, black and buff-white. The underparts are white with black barring. The eyes are dark brown, the legs and feet yellow. The female has thin black stripes above and below the eye and from the corners of the gape in a downward le across the throat. The breast is light ochre and lacks any barring. Immature birds are similar to adult females but are paler and have more rufous and buff-brown feathering. Usually encountered in pairs or small parties searching areas of short grass for seeds, beetles, ants and other small invertebrates. Resident. Size 25 cms.

Crested Francolin
(Francolinus sephae...

An inhabitant of thick bush and woodlands with sparse ground cover, usually in the vicinity of water. The crown is dark brown-black, the eye and moustachial stripes are black. The neck is white-buff heavily blotched with dark brown. The back and wing feathers are brown-grey edged with buff-white. The tail is black with much brown and grey flecking. The breast, belly and underparts are buff-rufous brown streaked with white. The eyes are dark brown and the legs and feet pink-red. The bill is black. The sexes are similar, the female having more cryptic plumage and being slightly smaller. Immatures are like females but usually paler They are usually encountered in pairs or small parties scratching around in the leaf litter for insects and larvae, seeds, berries and other plant material. They soo become very tolerant of man, if left unmolested, and often scavenge around bush camps. Resident. Size 27 cms.

Jackson's Francolin
(Francolinus jackson...

An endemic resident of the mountain forests of Kenya between 2200 and 3700 metres where they are quite abundant. A large francolin with a grey-brown head. The breast and belly feathers are rich chestnut edged with off-white. The mantle is grey-brown, the wing coverts and primary feathers are rufous brown. The tail is chestnut. The eyes are dark brown, the bill rich red and the legs and feet are bright red, the backs of the legs are darker. The sexes are similar, the female being slightly smaller than the male. Immature birds are generally darker in appearance and have dark brown barring on the wings and tail. In some areas within the Aberdares National Park they have become very tame and often frequent picnic sites and lodge grounds on the look out for food scraps. Resident. Size 38 cms.

Red-necked Francolin
(Francolinus afe...

A bird of wooded grasslands, having a distinctive bright red throat patch. The crown is dark grey-brown, the neck, breast and belly are grey-brown heavily and boldly blotched with black. The mantle and wings are olive brown streaked with black. The tail is brown with fine black barring. The eyes are dark brown surrounded by bright red areas of bare skin. The bill, legs and feet are bright red. The sexes are similar, the female being slightly smaller than the male. Immature birds have dull brown plumage, brown bill and the wing feathers streaked and barred with grey. They roost in trees, descending to the ground at dawn to forage for food among the leaf litter, taking mainly grass shoots, seeds, roots, berries and a variety of insects and larvae. Often located as a result of hearing the loud raucous call. Resident. Size 36 cms.

Grey-breasted Francolin
(Francolinus rufopio...

Restricted in distribution to north-west Tanzania where they inhabit woodlands a thickets along river edges, venturing into surrounding grasslands only in the early morning and late afternoon. The crown and nape are dark brown-black with some light flecking, the neck is blackish with streaks of grey. The back and wing coverts are chestnut with grey and black streaking. The primary and secondary wing feathers are grey-brown with buff edging. The tail is grey with black barring and flecking. The breast is grey with black streaking, the belly and underparts are ligh grey streaked with black and buff. The eyes are dark brown surrounded by an area bright orange-pink unfeathered skin. The moustachial stripes and eyebrows are white. The bill and throat patch are orange. The legs and feet are dark, almost blac At a distance they may be confused with Red-necked Francolin (*Francolinus afer*) but the throat patch of orange and legs of black ease identification. The sexes are similar, the females being slightly smaller. They can be found singly, in pairs or in small parties foraging among grass and leaf litter for seeds and insects. Resident. S 36 cms.

Yellow-necked Spurfowl
(Francolinus leucoscep...

A very common species throughout much of the region, an inhabitant of open country, dry bush and woodland and forest edges. The crown and nape are brown-black with some fine flecking. The hindneck is brown-black with bold white streak The throat patch of bare unfeathered skin is bright pale yellow. The upperparts, breast and belly are dark brown heavily blotched and streaked with chestnut and buff-white. The primary and secondary wing feathers are grey-brown with fine bla speckling, in flight a pale patch on the wings is conspicuous.The tail is brown with fine grey flecking. The eyes are dark brown surrounded by patches of pink-red unfeathered skin. The bill is blue-grey to black and the legs and feet brownish-blac The sexes are similar, the female being slightly smaller than the male. They roost o the ground in trees and bushes descending at daybreak to forage singly, in pairs or small parties for seeds and insects. Resident. Size 36 cms.

Helmeted Guineafowl
(Numida meleagr...

Common throughout the region in open grasslands with scattered bush, along woodland edges and on cultivated farmland. The head and neck are unfeathered an boldly marked with bright red on the forehead, around the base of the bill and on th lower cheeks. The sides of the face and neck are bright powder blue. On the crown i a reddish-orange casque of variable size. The hindneck has a line of short, spiky black feathers and the throat and foreneck are black. The plumage of both upper and underparts is dark brown-black with white spots, the spots being smaller and more concentrated on the lower neck, breast and back becoming larger towards the rear. The primary and secondary wing feathers are dark brown-black with white bars rather than spots. The eyes are dark brown. The bill is dull yellow-orange, the legs and feet brownish black. The sexes are similar, the female being slightly smaller tha the male. They roost above the ground in trees and spend the daytime foraging in large flocks feeding on seeds, roots and a variety of insects including grasshoppers and termites. Resident. Size 56 cms.

Vulturine Guineafowl
(Acryllium vulturinum

The most handsome of East Africa's guineafowl species found in arid areas of Kenya Somalia, south-eastern Ethiopia and north-west Tanzania. The head and neck are blue-grey and unfeathered with the exception of a collar of dull chestnut feathers around the nape. The breast and mantle feathers are long and loose, striped black, white and rich cobalt blue. The back and wings are black evenly spotted with white. The primary wing feathers are brown-black edged with white and the secondaries are brown-black edged with violet. The black and white spotted tail is long, with the central feathers often trailing along the ground. The eyes are bright red, the bill pale grey and the legs and feet grey-black. The sexes are alike. They feed usually in large flocks ,on seeds, berries, fruits and a variety of insects. Resident. Size 60 cms.

Crowned Crane
(Balearica regulor

A large long legged bird of open grasslands, lakes, swamps and farmland. The forehead and fore-crown are black, the hind-crown and nape have a stiff crest of golden yellow feathers. The neck is light grey with loose feathers at the base trailing onto the breast and mantle. The upperparts are black. The wing coverts are buff-white to golden yellow, the secondary wing feathers are black and chestnut, the primaries are glossy black. The breast is grey-black with long, loose feathering on upper portion, the belly and underparts are dark grey-black. The cheeks are white with a red flash extending along the sides of the hind-crown. The throat has a bright red wattle. The eyes are pale blue and the bill, legs and feet are black. The sexes are similar, the crest is less developed in the female. Resident. Size 102 cms.

Black Crake
(Amaurornis flavirost

A shy but common species throughout the region, frequenting areas of dense reed and vegetation in swamps, marshes and around the margins of lakes and ponds. The plumage is entirely blue-black, with the eyes and orbital ring bright red. The bill is yellow and the legs, feet and long toes are bright pinkish-red. The sexes are alike. Immature birds have a plumage of olive brown, the bill is dull yellow-green, the eyes are orange-red and the legs and feet dull blood red. Often seen foraging around the waters edge taking insects from the water surface as well as preying on snails, small fish and amphibians. Resident. Size 20 cms.

Moorhen
(Gallinula chloropu

Common throughout much of the region, inhabiting freshwater lakes, swamps, marshes, streams and rivers. The head and neck are blue-black becoming slaty blue on the mantle, breast and belly. A conspicuous white streak is visible along the flanks. The wing coverts and flight feathers show variable amounts of brown-black. The tail is black with undertail coverts a prominent white particularly when the tail is flicked upwards in alarm. The bill is bright red at the base and has a bright yellow tip. An unfeathered shield extends from the base of the bill upwards over the forehead and onto the fore-crown. The legs and feet are yellowish-green with an orange-red band on the upper leg. The eyes are red to dark brown. The sexes are alike, the shield being less well developed in the female. Resident. Size 33 cms.

Purple Gallinule
(Porphyrio porphyri

Found over much of East Africa in swamps, marshes and reedbeds. The head, neck and mantle are purple-blue. The plumage of both upper and underparts is iridescent purple with a wash of green on the back. The face and throat have a wash of light blue. The rump and tail are bronze-blue, the under tail coverts are white. The primary and secondary wing feathers are blackish-purple. The bill and frontal head shield are rich red, the eyes are deep blood red and the legs, feet and long toes are pinkish-red. The sexes are alike. Resident. Size 46 cms.

Red-knobbed Coot
(Fulica cristata

An inhabitant of open freshwater lakes, ponds and flood plains, often forming into large flotillas. The entire plumage is black with washes of brown on the rump and tail and with some grey on the underside. The bill and frontal shield is white often having a faint blue wash. At the apex of the shield are found two circular red knobs, these knobs become greatly reduced in size during periods of non-breeding. The eyes are dark rich red, the legs and feet darkish grey. The sexes are alike. Immature birds are dark brown above and pale grey below, with a variable amount of white on the throat and neck. They feed mainly on aquatic plant material as well as grasses, seeds, snails and insects. Resident. Size 40 cms.

Kori Bustard
(Ardeotis k...

The largest of East Africa's bustards found in areas of open savannah, lightly wood... grasslands and dry bush country. The crown is black with a short crest extending from the rear. The face and neck are mid-grey finely barred with black, the mantle... black. The back and flight feathers are grey-brown finely marked with light and da... grey. The breast, belly and underparts are white. The wing coverts are white, often with a tinge of buff, broadly marked with black. The eyes are dull yellow, the bill is... grey with a wash of yellow, and the legs and feet are light grey. The sexes are simila... the female being smaller than the male. Usually encountered singly or in pairs walking in grassland areas feeding on disturbed insects, reptiles and small rodents... During courtship the male displays, to attract a female, by fanning and lifting the ta... dropping the wing tips to the ground and inflating the neck into a large whitish bal... Resident. Size 100 cms.

Buff-crested Bustard
(Eupodotis ruficrist...

A small bustard of dry thornbush, lightly wooded areas and open arid plains. The crown is buff-grey forming an erect crest during courtship and often when alarmed... The face and upper neck are soft orange-brown, the lower neck greyish becoming white on the upper breast. A black line extends from the chin down the centre of th... throat and neck to the black breast, belly and underparts. The feathers of the back and wings have a mottled appearance of buff, black and grey. The tail is greyish brown, the eyes are pale yellow, the bill dark grey and the legs and feet pale yellow-grey. The female differs from the male in being paler and having the crown brown and in lacking the black chin to breast stripe. Resident. Size 52 cms.

White-bellied Bustard
(Eupodotis senegalensi...

A bird of open grasslands, arid bush and lightly wooded savannahs. The male has a black forehead and crown becoming blue-grey towards the rear. The face is white with black stripes extending from the base of the upper mandible across the upper cheek to a point below the eye and from the chin around the upper throat onto the sides of the blue-grey neck. The upperparts are rufous-buff streaked and finely barred with dark brown. The breast is grey and the belly and underparts are white. The eyes are brown, the bill pink to yellow and the legs and feet pale yellow. The female is smaller than the male and lacks the dark crown, the black facial stripes and the blue-grey neck. Resident. Size 60 cms.

Black-bellied Bustard
(Eupodotis melanogaster...

An inhabitant of open areas of tall grassland and sparsely wooded savannahs. The forehead and crown are black flecked with tawny-buff. The face is grey with a black stripe extending from the eye to the nape. The neck is grey to tawny-buff, a broad black stripe, edged with white, runs from the chin down the centre of the throat and neck to the black breast and underparts. The back and wings are tawny-buff heavily blotched and streaked with brown-black. The tail is buff-brown with dark brown bands. The eyes are brown, the bill, legs and feet dull yellow. The female differs from the male in having the chin white, the throat buff and underparts of grey-white. Resident. Size 60 cms.

Hartlaub's Bustard
(Eupodotis hartlaubii...

This species can easily be confused with the Black-bellied Bustard having similar plumage and occurring in the same types of habitat, although Hartlaub's often favours drier regions. The plumage is generally greyer than that of the Black-bellied and the rump and tail are black. A broad, well defined, black band extends from the chin to the breast and from the eye to the nape. The jet black plumage of the breast and underparts arcs around the wings onto the shoulders. The female has all white breast and underparts, the foreneck, throat and chin are white and she lacks the head markings of the male. Found singly or in small groups and feeds on a wide variety of insects and vegetation. Resident. Size 60 cms.

African Jacana
(Actophilornis africa...)

Common throughout the region, frequenting areas of open water with an abundan... of aquatic vegetation. The crown, nape and hindneck are black. A pale blue area o... bare skin forms a frontal shield on the forehead. The chin, cheeks, throat and foreneck are white. The remaining plumage of both upper and underparts is chestnut brown. The eyes are dark brown, the bill is blue-grey and the legs and fee... dull grey-brown. The toes are extremely long, spreading the birds weight as it walk... on floating vegetation in search of insect food. The sexes are similar, the female bei... larger than the male. Resident. Size 28 cms.

Spotted Stone Curlew
(Burhinus capen...)

Widespread throughout East Africa in savannah and grassland areas with bush and light tree cover, often around kopjes in the Serengeti and on arid stony hill sides. T... plumage is pale buff to tawny brown heavily blotched and streaked with dark brown-black. The eyebrows, underparts and thighs are white. The bill is yellow at the base, tipped with black. The legs and feet are bright yellow. The large yellow ey... are very prominent. The sexes are alike. They are mainly active at night, being foun... during the daytime, usually in pairs or small flock, in communal roosts around scattered bushes. Resident. Size 42 cms.

Water Dikkop
(Burhinus vermiculat...)

An inhabitant of lake side margins, riverbanks, estuaries and beaches. The crown, hindneck, mantle, back and wing coverts are grey-brown flecked and streaked with... dark brown-black. The lower wing coverts are black at the base forming a distinct wing bar. The primary wing feathers are black. The eyebrows and cheeks are white as is the chin. The throat and breast are buff-white streaked with dark brown. The belly and underparts are white. The large prominent eyes are pale yellow. The bill i... black with a yellowish tinge at the base, the legs and feet are pale yellow-green The sexes are alike. Active mainly at night when they feed on molluscs and insects. Resident. Size 36 cms.

Long-toed Lapwing
(Vanellus crassirostr...)

Found around lakes and ponds with floating aquatic vegetation. The forehead, fore-crown, face, chin and throat are white contrasting strongly with the black hind-crown, nape, hindneck, mantle and breast. The belly and underparts are white. The upperparts are grey-brown, the upper wing coverts are white being very conspicuou... in flight. The tail is black with a white band at the base. The eyes are red with a crimson orbital ring. The bill is pinkish-red at the base, tipped with black, the legs, feet and long toes are dull red. The sexes are alike. Resident. Size 30 cms.

Blacksmith Plover
(Vanellus armatu...)

An inhabitant of lake edges, swamps, marshes and riverbanks. The forehead and crown are white. The hind-crown, nape, face, chin, neck and breast are black. The hindneck, belly and underparts are white. The back and outer scapulars are black, the inner scapulars and wing coverts are silver-grey. The primary and secondary wing feathers are black, the rump and tail are white the latter having a terminal band of black. The eyes are a rich dark red, the bill, legs and feet are black. The sexes are alike. Resident. Size 28 cms.

Spur-winged Plover
(Vanellus spinosus...)

A common and widespread species particularly in Uganda, Ethiopia, Somalia and Kenya inhabiting open bare ground around lakes, along riverbanks, on estuaries, beaches and soda flats. The upper portion of the head from a point below the eye is black. The lower portion of the head and the sides and back of the neck are white. The chin, throat, breast and upper belly are black, the remaining underparts are white. The mantle, back and wing coverts are greyish-brown, the primary wing feathers are black. The eyes are dark red, the bill, legs and feet are black. The sexes are alike. Resident. Size 27 cms.

Blackhead Plover
(Vanellus tect...)

A bird of open arid grasslands and bare ground near lakes, ponds and rivers. The forehead and chin are white. The crown is black and has a short crest. A thick band of white extends from behind the eye widening to cover the nape. A black collar extends from the hindneck to the upper throat, broadening to the base of the eye, from the throat it runs down the centre of the neck and breast. The sides of the breast and the underparts are white. The upperparts and wing coverts are grey-brown. The primary and secondary wing feathers are black. The tail is white with a terminal black band. The eyes are bright yellow, the bill dull red with a black tip and the legs and feet red. The sexes are alike. Resident. Size 25 cms.

Senegal Plover
(Vanellus lugubr...)

A long legged, slender plover of open savannahs and burnt grassland areas. The forehead is white, the remainder of the head is brownish-grey. The chin is white, the neck and throat light grey. The upperparts and wing coverts are brownish-grey, the secondary wing feathers are white and the primaries black. The tail is white tipped with black. The upper breast is grey, darkening to form a black band above the white belly and underparts. The eyes are golden yellow, the bill, legs and feet black. The sexes are alike. Resident. Size 25 cms.

Black-winged Plover
(Vanellus melanopter...)

A species usually found on grasslands above 2100 metres. The forehead, fore-crown and chin are white. The hind-crown and nape are grey-blue, the neck light grey becoming lighter in the region of the throat. Across the upper breast is a broad black band. The lower breast, and underparts are white. The upperparts are greyish-brown, the greater wing coverts are white. The secondary wing feathers are white at the base and black at the tips, the primaries are all black. The tail is white with a black band towards the tip. The eyes are yellow contrasting with a red orbital ring. The bill is dark grey-blue and the legs and feet are dull red. The female is browner and has a less distinct, white forehead patch. Resident. Size 28 cms.

Crowned Plover
(Vanellus coronatu...)

A common plover in areas of short grass savannahs and open plains. The forehead is black from which a stripe extends around the head to the nape. Above this, around the base of the black crown, runs a white band. The chin is white and the cheeks, neck, upper breast and mantle are grey-brown becoming lighter on the throat and foreneck. The upperparts and wing coverts are a slightly darker grey-brown and the primary and secondary wing feathers are white at the base and black at the tips. The tail is white with a black band towards the base. The breast is grey-brown darkening to form a narrow black band on the lower breast. The belly and underparts are white. The eyes are bright yellow, the bill is pinkish-red at the base and black towards the tip. The legs and feet are bright red. The sexes are alike. Resident. Size 28 cms.

Wattled Plover
(Vanellus senegallus...)

Usually found in the vicinity of water. A long legged, upright plover with a white forehead. The crown and hindneck are dark olive-brown finely speckled with brown-black. The cheeks, throat and foreneck are whitish heavily streaked with dark brown. The back and wing coverts are olive-brown and the tail is white. The chin and upper throat are black, the breast is buff and the underparts are white. The primary wing feathers are black. The eyes are pale yellow with a bright yellow orbital ring. At the base of the bill are situated bright red and yellow wattles. The legs and feet are golden yellow. The sexes are alike. Resident. Size 33 cms.

Kittlitz's Plover
(Charadris pecuarius...)

A very small plover, well distributed throughout the region. Found on bare areas of ground around lakes and along river banks and tidal mudflats. The forehead is black, the fore-crown is black the hind-crown brown flecked with buff. A white band extends from above the eye to the nape and a black band extends from the base of the bill, through the eye to the mantle. The feathers of the upperparts and wing coverts are greyish-brown edged with buff. The lower cheeks, chin and throat are white. The breast is buff-yellow and the underparts are white. The eyes are dark brown, the bill, legs and feet are black. The sexes are similar. Resident. Size 14 cms.

Ringed Plover
(Charadrius hiatic

A winter visitor to coastal regions, inland lakes and river banks. The forehead is white, the fore-crown is black with the top and hind-crown olive brown. A black band extends from the base of the bill, through the eye, linking with the black fore crown, then on across the cheeks to the sides of the nape. A black collar runs from the mantle around and across the upper breast. The lower breast and underparts a white. The back and wing coverts are olive-brown, the primary wing feathers are brown-black. The contrasting black and white plumage of the head and neck is mu reduced during the winter months. The eyes are dark brown with a yellow-orange orbital ring. The bill is red tipped with black (blackish during winter). The legs an feet are orange-red. The sexes are similar. Resident. Size 19 cms.

Little-ringed Plover
(Charadrius dubi

A palearctic winter visitor to the margins of freshwater lakes, rivers and less commonly coastal regions. The forehead is white. The fore-crown, the sides of the face and head to the sides of the nape, are black. The remainder of the crown is brown. A broad black band extends from the mantle around and across the upper breast. The lower breast and underparts are white. The back and wing coverts are brown, the primaries are blackish. The eyes are brown with a bright yellow orbital ring. The bill is black and the legs and feet are yellow-grey. The sexes are similar. Palearctic winter visitor. Size 15 cms.

Three-banded Plover
(Charadrius tricollar

A small plover encountered around the shores of lakes and ponds, on river banks and sand bars. Uncommon in coastal areas. The forehead is white, the crown and nape dark brown. A white stripe extends from above the eye around the crown to th nape. The chin, throat and face are greyish. Two black bands extend across the uppe and lower breast separated by a band of white. The underparts are white. The back and wings are olive brown. The eyes are honey yellow with a bright red orbital ring. The bill is red at the base and black at the tip. The legs and feet are dull blood red. The sexes are alike. Resident. Size 18 cms.

Chestnut-banded Sand Plover
(Charadrius pallidus

Found only on the alkaline lakes of northern Tanzania and southern Kenya. The forehead and narrow eyebrows are white. The crown is dark chestnut-black at the fore and greyish brown elsewhere. A thin black stripe extends from the base of the bill to the eye. The cheeks, chin and throat are white with a wash of pale chestnut on the upper cheeks. The underparts are white with the exception of a broad chestnut band which extends across the upper breast. The mantle, back and wing coverts are greyish-brown. The primary wing feathers are brown-black. The eyes are dark brown, the bill is black and the legs and feet greenish-grey. The sexes are similar. Resident. Size 15 cms.

Caspian Plover
(Charadrius asiaticus

An abundant winter visitor from Asia, often found in large flocks on short grasslands. Usually having non-breeding plumage when the forehead, chin, throat, sides of neck and eye stripe are buff-white. The crown is greyish brown. The hindneck, sides of the lower neck and breast are buff flecked with grey-brown. The feathers of the mantle, back and wing coverts are tawny- brown edged with buff. The primary wing feathers are brown-black. Some birds may arrive for the winter and depart for the breeding grounds in spring having attained breeding plumage, when the face and foreneck are white and a rich chestnut breast band develops. The sexes are similar, the plumage of the female being generally duller. Palearctic winter visitor. Size 20 cms.

Avocet
(Recurvirostra avosetta)

A bird of both freshwater and alkaline lakes, mudflats, flood plains and estuaries. The head and hindneck are black. The chin, cheeks, throat, foreneck, breast and underparts are white. The back, rump, tail and secondary wing feathers are white, the wing coverts and primaries black. The thin upturned bill which is specially adapted for feeding is black. The legs and feet are pale blue. The sexes are similar, the female occasionally having areas of black plumage tinged brown. A resident and palearctic winter visitor. Size 43 cms.

Black-winged Stilt
(Himantopus himant

A widely distributed species, found in shallow waters, both fresh and alkaline, marshes, esturies and coastal mudflats. The head, neck, breast, underparts and t are white, in breeding plumage the head and neck show a variable amount of dar grey-black. The wings are black. The eyes are deep red. The long thin bill is black The bright pink-red legs are extremely long, extending beyond the tail in flight. T sexes are similar, the female usually showing a hint of brown on the mantle and scapulars. Resident and palearctic winter visitor. Size 38 cms.

Crab Plover
(Dromas ard

A visitor to the coastal areas of Kenya and Tanzania from September to March. Th head, neck, breast, underparts, back and scapulars are white, during non-breedin periods the crown, nape and hindneck are flecked and streaked with grey. The mantle and primary and secondary flight feathers are brown-black. The eyes are o brown and the broad heavy bill is black. The legs and feet are pale blue-grey. The sexes are alike. Winter visitor. Size 35 cms.

Painted Snipe
(Rostratula benghaler

A bird of lakes, marshes and swamps with dense banks of vegetation. In this speci the female has the bright colourful plumage. The forehead and crown are dark bro with a buff central stripe extending to the nape. The eyes are surrounded by patch of white which extend towards the nape. The chin, throat and upper neck are rich dark chestnut, the lower neck and upper breast are dark chestnut graduating to bla on the lower breast. The underparts and sides of the breast around the wings are white. The wings and upperparts are dark green-bronze blotched and barred with black. The eyes are dark brown, the long slightly decurved bill is reddish brown an the legs and feet are greenish-yellow. The male lacks the rich plumage coloration o the female, having head and neck grey-buff streaked with brown, the breast is barre with brown and the wings are heavily blotched and barred with buffs and browns. Resident. Size 27 cms.

African Snipe
(Gallinago nigripenn

A bird of swamps and flooded areas usually at altitudes in excess of 1500 metres. The head is buff with a series of dark brown stripes extending from bill to hindneck these stripes running along the sides of the crown, through the eyes and across the cheeks. The hindneck, throat and breast are buff heavily streaked with dark brown. The belly, flanks and underparts are white, the flanks being conspicuously barred with dark brown. The back is blackish-brown with buff flecking, the wing coverts and flight feathers are dark brown-black edged and barred with white and buff. The eyes are dark brown. The long straight bill is pinkish-brown and the legs and feet are brownish-green. Mainly nocturnal but also active at dawn and dusk feeding in areas of mud and shallow water. The sexes are alike. Resident. Size 28 cms.

Curlew Sandpiper
(Calidris ferruginea

An abundant palearctic winter visitor particularly to coastal estuaries and mudflats but also found around the muddy edges of inland lakes both freshwater and alkaline The forehead, crown and hindneck are grey-brown. The eyebrows, cheeks, throat, neck and underparts are white-buff. During the breeding season
the face, breast and some wing coverts are rich chestnut, a hint of which may show in non-breeding and transitional plumages. The mantle and wing coverts are grey-brown edged with buff-white. The primary and secondary wing feathers are blackish-brown edged with white. The eyes are dark brown, the long slightly decurved bill is black as are the legs and feet. The sexes are similar. Winter visitor. Size 19 cms.

Little Stint
(Calidris mi...

A small but common palearctic winter visitor to coastal mudflats, estuaries and muddy margins of inland waters. The forehead is white, the crown, hindneck an... ear coverts are grey-brown. A white stripe follows the line of the eyebrow. The fr... and sides of the neck, breast, belly and underparts are white with some fine grey flecking on the breast. The feathers of the upperparts are grey-brown edged with white. The primary and secondary wing feathers are brownish-black edged with white. The eyes are dark brown and the bill, legs and feet are black. The sexes are alike. Palearctic winter visitor. Size 13 cms.

Sanderling
(Calidris a...

A palearctic winter visitor to coastal beaches and occasionally to mudflats and inland waters. The forehead is white and the crown, hindneck and mantle are gre... with streaks of brown. The cheeks, neck, centre of the breast and underparts are p... white, the sides of the breast are washed and streaked with grey-brown. The alula... and primary and secondary wing feathers are blackish-brown. The wing coverts a... grey-brown edged with white. The eyes are dark brown, the bill, legs and feet are black. The sexes are similar. Very active feeders, usually in small flocks darting about feeding along the tideline. Palearctic winter visitor. Size 20 cms.

Ruff
(Philomachus pugn...

An abundant palearctic winter visitor throughout the region, favouring the surrounds of lakes, ponds, swamps and marshes only occasionally being found in... coastal habitats. The forehead, cheeks and neck are white. The crown, nape and hindneck are tawny brown with fine darker brown flecking. The breast, belly and underparts are white with a variable amount of tawny brown mottling. The feather... of the mantle and wing coverts are dark brown edged with buff-white. The primary and secondary wing feathers are blackish-brown. The eyes are dark brown and the bill brownish-black. The legs and feet are pale orange. In non-breeding plumage th... sexes are similar, during breeding periods the males develop a large and spectacul... ruff around the head and neck which is extremely variable in colour, ranging from white-ochre to purple-black and chestnut. Palearctic winter visitor. Size 23 cms.

Black-tailed Godwit
(Limosa limo...

A palearctic winter visitor usually in small flocks on marshes, lake sides, coastal estuaries, mudflats and lagoons. A large wader with long legs and an extremely lon... straight bill. The head, neck and breast are grey-brown slightly lighter on the cheek... foreneck and centre of the breast. The underparts are white with a grey wash on the flanks. The feathering of the mantle and wing coverts is grey-brown edged with buf... white. The secondary wing feathers are dark brown edged with buff and the primaries are brownish-black. The tail is white at the base, the remainder being black, tipped with a narrow band of white. The eyes are dark brown, the long straig... bill is reddish-pink at the base becoming black at the tip. The legs and feet are black The sexes are similar. Palearctic winter visitor. Size 41 cms.

Bar-tailed Godwit
(Limosa lapponic...

A palearctic winter visitor to coastal estuaries, mudflats and the muddy margins of inland lakes. Very similar in general size and shape to the Black-tailed Godwit (*Limosa limosa*) but has shorter legs, a heavily barred brown and white tail and the suggestion of an upturned bill. The forehead, crown and hindneck are greyish-brown streaked with dark brown. The chin, face and throat are white finely marked with grey-brown. The breast has a wash of pale tawny brown and the underparts are white. The wing coverts are greyish-brown streaked with dark brown and edged with white. The primary and secondary wing feathers are blackish-brown, the secondaries being edged with white. The eyes are dark brown. The bill is black at the tip and pinkish-red towards the base. The legs and feet are blackish. Palearctic winter visitor. Size 38 cms.

Turnstone
(Arenaria inter

A winter visitor to coastal beaches and rocky shorelines, occasionally encountere
on the surrounds of inland waters. The forehead, crown and hindneck are grey-
brown streaked with dark brown. The face, cheeks, chin and upper neck are off-
white. The lower neck and upper breast are heavily marked with blackish-brown
The lower breast and underparts are white. The feathers of the mantle, scapulars
wing coverts are dark brown edged with buff and tawny brown. The primary win
feathers are white at the base and blackish-brown at the tips, the secondaries are
white which show as a conspicuous wing bar in flight. The tail is white at the bas
tipped with a broad black band. The eyes are dark brown, the bill is black and the
legs and feet bright orange. The sexes are similar. Usually encountered in small
flocks foraging among the rocks and debris along the tideline in search of insects
molluscs. Palearctic winter visitor. Size 23 cms.

Greenshank
(Tringa nebula

A bird of coastal mudflats and sandbars, the muddy surrounds of inland lakes bot
freshwater and alkaline, and exposed ground along river banks. The forehead,
crown, nape and hindneck are greyish-white streaked with dark brown. The chin,
face, breast and underparts are pure white with some fine dark brown streaking or
the cheeks and across the breast. The feathers of the upperparts and wing coverts a
greyish-brown, barred, blotched and streaked with dark brown and edged with
white. The tail is white with brown-black barring, the rump and centre of the back
are white, forming a distinctive wedge shape in flight. The secondary wing feather
are greyish-brown and the primaries are brownish-black. The eyes are dark brown.
The long slightly upturned bill is grey-green at the base and black at the tip. The le
and feet are greenish-yellow. The sexes are alike. They are normally solitary but m
form into flocks during migration. They usually depart for their breeding grounds
March or April with some birds returning as early as July. Palearctic winter visitor.
Size 31 cms.

Redshank
(Tringa totan.

A palearctic winter visitor mainly to coastal estuaries, mudflats and lagoons. A bir
of uniform grey-brown appearance. The head, face and neck are brown with fine
darker brown streaking, the sides of the face and neck are often paler. The throat,
breast and flanks are white streaked with brown, the belly and underparts are whit
The feathers of the mantle and wing coverts are brown with fine barring and
streaking. The back, rump and secondary wing feathers are white. The primary flig
feathers are dark brown. The tail is white finely barred with brown. The eyes are
dark brown contrasting with a white orbital ring. The long bill is orange-red at the
base and black towards the tip. The legs and feet are bright orange-red. The sexes ar
alike. They are often found feeding singly or in small flocks gathering together into
larger flocks during periods of migration. When flushed they will usually utter a
strident call, the wing beats are short and jerky. Palearctic winter visitor.
Size 28 cms.

Spotted Redshank
(Tringa erythropu

A wader that favours freshwater and alkaline inland lakes, pools and marshes. The
forehead, crown, nape and mantle are grey-brown. The eyebrow stripe, face and
neck are white, a dark brown stripe extends from the base of the bill through the eye
towards the nape. The breast is white with a mottling of grey-brown. The belly and
underparts are white. The feathers of the wing coverts are grey-brown edged with
white and the primary wing feathers are brownish-black. The rump and tail are
white, the latter finely barred with black. The eyes are dark brown with a white
orbital ring, the bill has the upper mandible all black and the lower mandible orange
red at the base and black towards the tip. The long legs and feet are bright orange-red
The sexes are alike. The breeding plumage, which some birds acquire before
migrating to the northern breeding grounds, is almost entirely black with white
spotting on the wings and flanks. The back and rump remain white. Palearctic
winter visitor. Size 30 cms.

Common Sandpiper
(Actitis hypole...)

A common palearctic winter visitor to coastal regions and inland waters. The forehead, crown and cheeks are olive brown streaked with dark brown. The upperparts and wings are olive brown finely barred with dark brown. The chin a... throat are white with a wash of buff, the upper breast is olive brown with fine da... brown streaking. The remainder of the breast, belly and underparts are white. Th... white feathering extends onto the sides of the breast arcing around the line of the... folded wings. The eyes are dark brown, the bill is grey-brown, the legs and feet p... greyish-yellow. The sexes are alike. Palearctic winter visitor. Size 20 cms.

Marsh Sandpiper
(Tringa stagna...)

A palearctic winter visitor to coastal mudflats, inland lakes, rivers and flood plai... The forehead is white, the crown, nape and hindneck are buff-grey streaked with dark brown. The face, throat, foreneck, breast, belly and underparts are white. Th... mantle and scapulars are tawny-buff streaked with dark brown. The wing coverts... grey-brown, the back and rump are white. The primary wing feathers are brown-black. The eyes are dark brown, the long slender bill is grey-black, the legs and fee... are greenish-yellow. The sexes are alike. Palearctic winter visitor. Size 23 cms.

Green Sandpiper
(Tringa ochro...)

A bird of freshwater lakes, ponds, rivers and streams throughout the region. The forehead and crown are olive brown heavily streaked with dark brown. The hindneck, sides of the neck and upper breast are whitish streaked and flecked wit... brown. The lower breast, belly and underparts are white. The wing coverts and primary and secondary wing feathers are dark olive brown barred and spotted wit... white. The tail is white with black barring, the rump white contrasting strongly w... the dark wings when seen in flight. The eyes are dark brown, the bill is greenish-yellow at the base and black at the tip. The legs and feet are greenish-grey. The sex... are alike. Palearctic winter visitor. Size 23 cms.

Wood Sandpiper
(Tringa glare...)

An abundant palearctic winter visitor to wetland areas. The forehead and eyebrow... are white, the crown is olive brown boldly streaked with dark brown. The hindnec... cheeks and upper breast are greyish with brown mottling. The lower breast, belly and underparts are white. The wing coverts and secondary wing feathers are olive brown edged with white, the primaries are dark olive brown. The tail is white barr... with black. The eyes are dark brown, the bill is blackish at the tip and yellow-green... at the base. The legs and feet are yellow-green. The sexes are alike. Palearctic winte... visitor. Size 20 cms.

Whimbrel
(Numenius phaeop...)

A large wader of coastal regions frequenting estuaries and rocky shorelines, occasional found on inland lakes. The forehead and crown have a buff central strip... with a dark brown stripe either side extending to the nape. A dark brown stripe run... from the base of the bill through the eye. The cheeks and the sides and back of the... neck are white streaked and flecked with dark brown. The chin, throat, foreneck an... breast are whitish-buff streaked with dark brown. The belly and underparts are white. The wing coverts and primary and secondary wing feathers are dark brown edged with buff and white. The eyes are dark brown, the long decurved bill is blackish often with pinkish-red at the base. The long legs and feet are grey-blue. Th... sexes are alike. Palearctic winter visitor. Size 40 cms.

Curlew
(Numenius arquat...)

A winter visitor to coastal mudflats and estuaries. A very large long legged wader with long decurved bill. The head, neck and breast are buff-white heavily streaked with dark brown. The belly and flanks are white, the latter with bold blackish-brow... streaks. The wing feathers are dark brown edged and tipped with buff-white, the primary flight feathers are brown-black. The eyes are dark brown, the bill is blackis... and the legs and feet are pale blue-grey. The sexes are alike. Palearctic winter visito... Size 58 cms.

Temminck's Courser
(Cursorius temmi[?]

A bird of short grasslands, dry bush savannah and cultivated farmland, often in [?] or small flocks. The crown is bright chestnut, the white eyebrows extend to the n[?] and a black stripe extends from the rear of the eyes to the nape and downward to hindneck. The neck, upper breast, mantle and upperparts are grey-brown. The lo[?] breast is chestnut becoming blackish towards the belly, the remainder of the underparts are white. The primary wing feathers are black and the secondaries g[?] brown. The eyes are dark brown, the slightly decurved bill is blackish. The legs a[?] feet are pale grey. The sexes are alike. A very upright bird, feeds by pecking then running a few steps before pecking again, collecting invertebrates and seeds as it does so. Resident. Size 20 cms.

Cream-coloured Courser
(Cursorius cu[?]

An inhabitant of arid semi-desert regions, cultivated farmland and bare stony are[?] A long legged, slender, upright bird with forehead and forecrown sandy rufous brown, the hindneck is grey-blue. The white eyebrows extend to the nape and downwards forming a 'V' at the top of the hindneck. A black stripe extends from t[?] rear of the eye to the hind-neck. The face, neck and throat are white with a wash o[?] buff on the cheeks. The breast is sandy-brown and the belly and underparts are white. The mantle, back and wing coverts are buff sandy-brown. The primary and[?] secondary wing feathers are black edged with buff. The eyes are dark brown, the decurved bill is black and the legs and feet are pale grey, almost white. The sexes a[?] alike. Similar to Temminck's Courser but lacks the dark breast band and the bright chestnut crown. Usually encountered in small flocks of up to 30 birds running around on bare, arid patches of ground feeding on disturbed insects, on small liza[?] and seeds, often scratching in the loose surface soil to expose ants etc. Resident. S[?] 23 cms.

Two-banded Courser
(Cursorius african[?]

A bird encountered on open bare patches of ground and short grassland areas, also[?] often seen along dirt roads. The crown is pale buff finely streaked with brown-blac[?] A black stripe extends from the base of the bill through the eye to the nape. The cheeks, chin and throat are buff-white, the neck is buff finely streaked and flecked with dark brown. The feathers of the back and wing coverts are sandy-brown with dark centres and broadly edged with white-buff. The rump is white and the tail bla[?] narrowly edged with white. The primary wing feathers are rufous brown to black and the secondaries are rufous to sandy-brown edged with white-buff. The upper breast is buff with a black band encircling the breast and mantle, a broader black band extends across the lower breast separated from the upper band by a band of sandy-buff. The lower breast, belly and underparts are whitish. The eyes are dark brown, the short bill is black and the legs and feet are pale grey. The sexes are alike. They are active mainly at dawn, dusk or through the night, when they feed on insec[?] especially termites. Resident. Size 20 cms.

Pratincole
(Glareola pratincol[?]

A resident and palearctic winter visitor to areas of open grassland, the surrounds of inland lakes and rivers as well as coastal regions. The crown, nape, face and sides and back of the neck are plain olive brown. The chin, throat and foreneck are creamy-yellow bordered by a narrow black band. The breast is buff-brown merging with white belly and underparts . The wing coverts are olive brown, the primary an[?] secondary wing feathers are black, the secondaries being tipped with white. The underwing coverts are chestnut which are conspicuous in flight. The rump is white and the tail black and deeply forked. The eyes are dark brown, the bill is black with red at the base, the legs and feet are blackish. During non-breeding periods the plumage is duller and the distinctive colour and markings of the throat and neck are[?] much reduced. The sexes are alike. Resident and palearctic winter visitor. Size 25 cms.

Grey-headed Gull

(Larus cirrocepha...)

A common gull on inland freshwater and alkaline lakes and along rivers. The forehead, crown, face, chin and upper throat are soft grey, the neck, lower throat, breast, belly and underparts are white with a faint wash of pink. The wing coverts and secondary wing feathers are grey, the primaries are black the outermost feathe... having distinctive white mirrors. The rump and tail are white. The eyes are pale yellow set in a bright red orbital ring. The bill is deep blood red and the legs and fe... are bright red. In non-breeding plumage the grey head becomes paler and the pink... flush is lost from the white feathering. The sexes are similar, the female being slightly smaller than the male. Usually encountered in flocks feeding from the surface of the water taking fish and insects, but will readily scavenge on rubbish ti... They will also take eggs and young from the nests of other waterbirds. Resident. Si... 40 cms.

European Lesser Black-back Gull

(Larus fusc...)

A winter migrant to coastal estuaries and shorelines as well as to inland lakes and rivers. The entire head, neck, breast, belly and underparts are white. The back and wing coverts are dark blue-black, the primary wing feathers are black, the outermo... primaries having white mirror spots. The eyes are pale yellow with a red orbital rin... the bill is yellow with a red patch on the lower mandible towards the tip. The legs and feet are yellow. The sexes are similar, the female being slightly smaller than the male. Immature birds have underparts streaked with dark brown, the feathers of the... upperparts are grey-brown edged with buff. The tail has a broad black band, the bill... is blackish, the eyes are dark brown and the legs and feet are dull pink. Adult plumage is not fully attained until the fourth summer, many first and second year birds remain in Africa even during the breeding season when adults fly north. Resident and palearctic winter visitor. Size 55 cms.

Black-headed Gull

(Larus ridibundu...)

A palearctic winter visitor to coastal estuaries and beaches, also encountered aroun... inland lakes and along open river banks, on newly ploughed farmland and scavenging on rubbish tips. In non-breeding plumage the head, neck, breast, belly and underparts are white, the head having smudge-like patches of black around the eyes and in the region of the ear coverts. The mantle, back and the majority of the wings are soft grey-blue. The primary wing feathers are white tipped with black. The rump and tail are white. The eyes are dark brown, the bill is dull red at the base with a black tip. The legs and feet are dull red. Immature birds are similar to non-breeding adults but have a broad black band across the tail and show brown feathering on the mantle and the tertials. The base of the bill is yellowish tipped with black and the legs and feet are yellow-pink. Many immature birds remain year round in the region. Resident and palearctic winter visitor. Size 38 cms.

Sooty Gull

(Larus hemprichii...)

A bird of coastal regions, rocky shores, beaches and mudflats. In breeding plumage the head and upper neck are dark brown-black, the lower neck and short eyebrows white. The mantle, back and wing coverts are brown-grey, the primary and secondary wing feathers are brown-black, the outer primaries being tipped with white. The breast and flanks are grey-brown, the belly, underparts and tail are white. The eyes are dark brown set in a red orbital ring. The bill is yellowish-green at the base with a black band before the red and yellow tip. The legs and feet are yellowish-green. In non-breeding plumage the colours of the head and the bare parts are much reduced, the whole plumage becoming greyer. The sexes are similar, the female being slightly smaller than the male. They feed on fish and other aquatic creatures as well as the eggs and chicks of other seabirds. Very rarely recorded inland. Resident. Size 45 cms.

Whiskered Tern
(Chlidonias hybrida)

A bird of freshwater and alkaline lakes and marshes. In breeding plumage the forehead, crown and nape are black, the chin and cheeks are white. the upperparts including the wing coverts are grey, the primary wing feathers are grey edged with dark grey-brown. The throat is pale grey becoming darker on the breast and almost black on the belly and flanks. The eyes are dark brown, the bill is red with a blackish tip and the legs and feet are bright red. In non-breeding plumage the black of the forehead, crown and nape is lost, becoming grey with streaks and smudges of black, the bill, legs and feet become dark brown-black. The sexes are similar. Resident and palearctic winter visitor. Size 25 cms.

White-winged Black Tern
(Chlidonias leucoptera)

An abundant palearctic winter visitor to the Rift Valley Lakes, rarely found on the coast. In non-breeding plumage the forehead is white, the crown and nape white streaked with grey-black. A smudge of black is present in the region of the ear coverts. The neck, breast and underparts are white. The upperparts including wing coverts and tail are pale grey. The eyes are dark brown, the bill blackish, often with trace of red at the base, the legs and feet are dull red. Between plumages they can appear quite piebald. The sexes are similar. Palearctic winter visitor. Size 24 cms.

Gull-billed Tern
(Gelochelidon nilotica)

An inhabitant of large inland lakes and rivers, coastal lagoons, estuaries and grassland plains. In breeding plumage the forehead, crown, nape and hindneck are black. The chin, cheeks, remainder of the neck, breast and underparts are white. The mantle and wing coverts are silver-grey, the primary wing feathers are grey edged with black. The eyes are dark brown, the substantial bill is black, the legs and feet blackish. In non-breeding plumage the bird is generally paler with the forehead, crown and nape white with a variable amount of black streaking. The area around the eyes is dark grey. The sexes are similar. Resident and palearctic winter visitor. Size 38 cms.

Caspian Tern
(Sterna caspia)

Found on coastal estuaries, beaches and rocky shorelines, on inland lakes and large rivers. A very large tern with forehead, crown and nape black, often with the impression of a short stiff crest on the hind-crown. The neck, breast and underparts are white. The mantle and wing feathers are pale soft-grey, the primary wing feathers are mid-grey edged with dark grey. The eyes are dark brown. The heavy bill is bright orange-red, the legs and feet black. In non-breeding plumage the forehead, crown and nape become white-grey with a variable amount of black streaking. Usually feeds singly or in small groups flying a few metres above the water surface from where they plunge-dive for fish. Resident. Size 53 cms.

African Skimmer
(Rhynchops flavirostris)

A bird found in the vicinity of large expanses of inland water and along the coastline of much of the region. Almost unmistakeable. The forehead, cheeks, sides and foreneck, breast and underparts are white. The crown, nape, hindneck, back and wing coverts are black-brown. The primary and secondary wing feathers are black-brown edged with buff and grey. The forked tail is white. The eyes are dark brown. The orange-red bill is specially adapted to suit the birds unusual feeding method, the upper mandible is shorter than the lower mandible by some 25 mm. When feeding the bird skims over the surface of the water using short buoyant wing beats, with the lower mandible held just below the surface, when a prey item is detected the shorter upper mandible instantly snaps shut. Resident. Size 35 cms.

Chestnut-bellied Sandgrouse

(Pterocles exust...)

A bird of dry semi-desert areas, open grasslands and thornbush country. The forehead, crown and hindneck are sandy-brown, the remainder of the head and ne... is yellow-ochre. The throat and upper breast are sandy-brown, a thin black band extends across the breast from the fold of the wings. Below this band the lower bre... becomes chestnut darkening to black on the belly and underparts. The scapulars a... wing coverts are yellow-ochre with some white spotting, edged with buff-white an... black. The primary and secondary wing feathers are dark brown, some of the primaries having white tips. The tail has long narrow central feathers. The eyes are dark brown set in a pale orbital ring. The bill is blue-grey and the legs and feet are blue-black. The female differs from the male in having the crown and hindneck streaked with dark brown, the breast spotted with dark brown and with narrow brown-black barring on the wings. The wing feathers also show more prominent sandy-buff spotting and barring. They feed in flocks mainly on seeds and plant material, but also take small quantities of beetles and other insects. Resident. Size 30 cms.

Black-faced Sandgrouse

(Pterocles decorat...)

An inhabitant of dry bush and semi-desert regions. The male has distinctive head markings consisting of a pale base to the upper mandible contrasting with a black forehead, chin and throat. The fore-crown is white and a white eye stripe, bordered below by a narrow black stripe, extends from the fore-crown to the sides of the nape. The crown, nape and hindneck are ochre streaked with black. The cheeks, sides of the neck and upper breast are buff-ochre, a black band extends across the breast below which the lower breast is white, the belly is dark brown. The feathers of the upperparts and wings are buff to ochre heavily streaked and barred with black-brown. The eyes are dark brown set in patches of bare yellow skin, the bill is orange-yellow and the legs and feet are dull orange. The female differs from the male in having no facial pattern, no eye stripe or breast band, the head and breast being streaked and barred with brown. Resident. Size 28 cms.

Lichtenstein's Sandgrouse

(Pterocles lichtensteini...)

Found in arid areas of hilly bush country, usually in pairs. The male has a white forehead and fore-crown separated by a broad band of black. The remainder of the crown and the nape are buff, heavily streaked with black. The chin and cheeks are buff-white with black speckling. The neck, throat and mantle are buff boldly barred with black. The breast is yellow-ochre broken by a narrow black band across the upper breast and a broader black band across the lower section. The belly and underparts are white with black barring. The back, rump and tail are buff-brown with black barring, the latter with a broad black band towards the yellow-ochre tip. The wing coverts, scapulars and secondary wing feathers are a mosaic of buff and ochre heavily blotched and barred with black and white. The primary wing feathers are black-brown narrowly edged with white. The eyes are dark brown surrounded by an area of bare pale yellow skin. The bill is orange-yellow, the legs and feet are yellow, the thighs are feathered white. The female lacks the bold head markings and breast bands of the male, having head and breast ochre-buff barred and streaked with black. Resident. Size 28 cms.

Yellow-throated Sandgrouse

(Pterocles gutturalis)

A bird of short grasslands usually close to water, encountered in pairs or small flocks. The male has the forehead, crown and nape olive brown and a creamy-yellow stripe extending from the base of the upper mandible to a point above and to the rear of the eye. The chin, throat and cheeks are creamy-yellow bordered below by a black band across the neck to the ear coverts. The lower neck and breast are plain dusky-buff, the belly and underparts are dark chestnut and black. The mantle and wing coverts are dusky-buff edged greyish, the primary wing feathers are dark brown-black edged with buff-white and the secondaries are olive-grey with a wash of chestnut brown. The eyes are dark brown set in an area of bare grey skin. The bill is slate-blue, the legs and feet brown. The female differs from the male in having the head, throat and neck buff-brown heavily streaked with dark brown, both upper and underparts are heavily spotted and barred with dark brown. Resident. Size 33 cms.

Speckled Pigeon
(Columba gu[?]

A widespread species throughout the region found in a variety of habitats includ[?] open grasslands, woodlands, rocky slopes and cliffs, cultivated farmland and around human settlements, cities and suburban gardens. The head and upper ne[?] are blue-grey, the eyes are surrounded by a large area of claret-red unfeathered sk[?] The neck and upper breast feathers are pale chestnut edged with grey. The breast, belly and underparts are plain blue-grey, the back and scapulars are chestnut. Th[?] wing coverts are chestnut boldly tipped with triangular white patches, the prima[?] wing feathers are greyish-brown. The eyes are pale golden-yellow, the bill is blac[?] with a white cere, the legs and feet are reddish-pink. The sexes are alike. They are usually found in small flocks of 4 - 6 birds but are sometimes encountered in floc[?] numbering several hundred feeding on the ground taking seeds, fruits and, when [?] season, many cultivated crops such as wheat, barley, millet and maize. Resident. Size 40 cms.

Red-eyed Dove
(Streptopelia semitorqu[?]

A common dove of woodland habitats usually close to water, forest edges, suburb[?] gardens and park land. The forehead is white becoming grey-blue on the crown an[?] nape. The sides of the head and neck are mauve with a wash of pink. At the base o[?] the nape is a black half collar that extends around the sides of the neck. The breast[?] belly and flanks are mauve-pink, the undertail coverts are greyish. The mantle, ba[?] and wings are brown, the primary wing feathers are dark brown finely edged with white. The eyes are orange-red surrounded by small patches of dark red unfeather[?] skin. The bill is blackish, the legs and feet are reddish-pink The sexes are alike. Usually found singly, in pairs or small flocks feeding on a variety of seeds, berries and fruits. Resident. size 30 cms.

Mourning Dove
(Streptopelia decipie[?]

A bird found over much of the region in acacia woodlands particularly those close [?] water, cultivated farmland, parks and suburban gardens. The forehead, crown and cheeks are blue-grey, the neck is mauve-pink with a distinctive black half collar extending from the hindneck around the sides of the neck, this collar has narrow white edging. The chin and throat are whitish, the breast is mauve-pink becoming greyish-white on the belly, flanks and undertail coverts. The mantle, back, rump ar[?] wing coverts are brown, the primary and secondary wing feathers are dark brown finely edged with buff-white. The eyes are yellow surrounded by a circular patch o[?] pink-red unfeathered skin. The bill is black and the legs and feet are pinkish-red. The sexes are alike. Usually forages alone or in small flocks, often in association w[?] other doves, eating grain, seeds, berries, fruits and occasionally some insects. Resident. Size 28 cms.

Ring-necked Dove
(Streptopelia capicol[?]

A very widespread dove found in a variety of habitats including acacia woodlands, dry thornbush, around human habitations and on cultivated farmland, parks and in[?] suburban gardens. The head is blue-grey, usually paler on the forehead and cheeks. The chin and throat are whitish-grey, the neck is grey with a flush of mauve-pink an[?] has a black half collar around the hindneck. The breast is mauve-grey, the belly and underparts pale grey-white. The mantle, scapulars and wing coverts are grey-brown[?] The tail is grey-brown above and black below. The primary and secondary wing feathers are dark brown finely edged with grey-white. The eyes are dark brown, the bill is black and the legs and feet are dull flesh-pink. The sexes are alike. Often feeds singly or in pairs and freely associates with other dove species foraging for seeds, plant material and occasionally invertebrates including earthworms and termites. They often gather in large flocks around waterholes during the dry season. Resident. Size 25 cms.

Laughing Dove
(Streptopelia senegale

A common and widespread dove throughout the region in areas of acacia woodla
and thornbush, cultivated farmland and around human habitations. The head an
upper neck are pale grey with a flush of pink. The foreneck has a broad half collar
rufous flecked with black. The breast is pinkish-grey becoming white on the belly
and underparts. The mantle and scapulars are rufous brown, the wing coverts are
greyish-blue, the primary wing feathers are brown-black and the secondaries are
blue-grey edged with black. The back and rump are blue-grey and the tail is brow
black. The eyes are dark brown, the bill is blue-black and the legs and feet are dull
red. The sexes are similar. Resident. Size 24 cms.

Namaqua Dove
(Oena caper

The smallest of East Africa's doves with a long pointed tail, found in areas of
thornbush and dry scrub, lightly wooded savannah and on cultivated farmland. T
male has the forehead, face, chin, throat and breast black, the remainder of the hea
and neck being pale grey. The belly and underparts are white. The mantle and bac
are grey-brown, the tail is brown-black. The wing coverts are pale grey, the primar
wing feathers are rufous brown edged with black and the secondaries are grey-bro
edged with black. The eyes are dark brown, the bill is reddish at the base and oran
yellow at the tip. The legs and feet are pinkish-red. The female differs from the ma
in lacking the black facial markings and breast bib, instead being pale grey-brown.
The primaries are grey-brown. Resident. Size 21 cms.

Emerald-spotted Wood Dove
(Turtur chalcospil

A small dove of woodlands, forests and cultivated farmland. The head is grey, the
nape and hindneck light-brown. The face and foreneck are greyish, the breast, bell
and underparts are buff-white with a wash of pink on the former. The mantle, back
and rump are brown, the wing coverts are brown with several large oblong metallic
green patches. The primary wing feathers are rufous brown, being very pronounce
in flight, tipped and edged with black-brown, the secondaries are dark brown-black
The eyes are dark brown, the bill is blackish and the legs and feet are dull pinkish-
red. The sexes are alike. Resident. Size 20 cms.

Green Pigeon
(Treron calv

A bird of woodlands, forests and cultivated farmland usually in the vicinity of fruit
trees particularly fig. The head, neck, breast, belly and underparts are yellow-green
The mantle, back, wing coverts and rump are olive-green, a patch of lilac-mauve
appears at the carpal joint of the folded wing. The primary and secondary wing
feathers are grey-brown edged with yellow. The eyes are pale blue-green, the bill is
pinkish-red with a grey tip and the legs and feet are bright pink-red. The sexes are
alike. Normally found in small parties feeding high in the canopy of fig and other
fruiting trees, where they are not easily spotted their plumage blending so well with
the foliage. They rarely feed on the ground occasionally doing so to feed on seeds.
Resident. Size 30 cms.

Olive Pigeon
(Columba arquatri

A bird of forests and woodlands mainly found at altitudes above 1400 metres. The
forehead and forecrown are purple, the hindcrown and nape are blue-grey. The
throat and neck are mauve-grey, the breast feathers are dark purple-red tipped with
white, the belly is maroon heavily spotted with white. The mantle is purple-brown
with some white spotting, the back and rump are dark brown. The wing coverts and
scapulars are maroon boldly spotted with white. The primary and secondary wing
feathers are dark brown, the tail is blackish. The eyes are brownish-yellow with a
bright yellow orbital ring. The bill, legs and feet are bright yellow. The sexes are
alike. Resident. Size 38 cms.

Orange-bellied Parrot

(Poicephalus rufiver...

A parrot of dry acacia woodland and thinly foliated trees particularly baobabs. The male has the head, neck and upper breast dusky-brown the cheeks and ear covert are finely streaked with white. The lower breast and belly are bright orange, the thighs and undertail coverts are bright yellow-green. The mantle, back and wing coverts are dusky-brown, the primary wing feathers and tail are brownish-black. eyes are dark orange-red surrounded by an area of dark brown unfeathered skin. bill, legs and feet are blackish. The female differs from the male in having lower breast and underparts yellow-green not orange. Usually found in small parties, the flight is fast during which they usually utter a shrill squawk. Resident. Size 25 cm

Brown Parrot

(Poicephalus mey...

Found in savannah woodlands. The head, neck and mantle are dark brown, the crown of the head bearing a pronounced band of yellow. The breast, belly and underparts are darkish blue-green, the thighs are yellow. The wing coverts are dar brown with the carpal area of the folded wing bright yellow. The primary wing feathers and tail are dark brown, the back and rump are bluish-green. The eyes are rich deep red surrounded by an area of black unfeathered skin. The bill, cere, legs and feet are blackish. The sexes are alike. They occur in pairs or small parties feed mainly on seeds, nuts and occasionally fruit. Resident. Size 25 cms.

Fischer's Lovebird

(Agapornis fisch...

Restricted in distribution to north western Tanzania and west to Rwanda and Burundi where they favour areas with acacia and baobab trees. The forehead, chee and chin are orange-red, the hindneck and breast are golden-yellow merging on th belly to yellow-green. The mantle and back are green, the uppertail coverts blue an the tail blue-green at the base permeating through yellow-green to a yellow tip wit black band on the outer feathers. The wing coverts are rich leaf green, the primary wing feathers dark green. The eyes are dark brown set in a prominent white orbital patch. The bill is bright red, the cere is white and the legs and feet are pinkish-grey. Resident. Size 14 cms.

Yellow-collared Lovebird

(Agapornis persona...

Restricted in distribution to a wide band extending north to south through cental Tanzania, inhabiting acacia woodlands and areas of baobab trees. Several feral populations have established themselves outside the normal breeding range on the Tanzanian coast. The head, chin and throat are dark brown. The nape, hindneck an breast are yellow, the belly and underparts are green. The mantle, back and wing coverts are green, the uppertail coverts are blue and the tail is green with a flush of orange and a black bar towards the tip. The primary wing feathers are green-brown. The eyes are dark brown with a pronounced white orbital patch, the bill is red with whitish cere, the legs and feet are grey. The sexes are alike. Resident. Size 15 cms.

Fischer's Lovebird / Yellow-collared Lovebird Hybrid

Fischer's Lovebird and Yellow-collared Lovebirds hybridize and several populatio are well established within the region, the principle locations being Nairobi and Lake Naivasha in Kenya. The forehead is reddish-peach, the crown and face are darkish-brown merging with the bright yellow nape, neck and breast, the latter ofte with a flush of orange. The belly and underparts are bright yellow-green. The back i yellow-green becoming blue-green on the rump and uppertail coverts. The wing coverts are dark green and the primary wing feathers are brownish. The eyes are dark brown, the bill is bright red with a narrow white cere and the legs and feet are grey. The sexes are alike. Resident. Size 14 cms.

Hartlaub's Turaco
(Tauraco hartlar

A common turaco of highland forests in Kenya and Tanzania. The forehead, crown and nape feathers are dark blue and take the form of a fan-shaped crest. A white patch appears in front of the eye which is surrounded by a red orbital ring. A white stripe extends from below and to the rear of the eye to the ear coverts. The sides of the face, chin, throat, neck and breast are leaf green. The belly and underparts are greyish-black. The mantle, back and wing coverts are green becoming dark blue on the secondary wing feathers. The primary wing feathers are edged with rich red. The tail is dark blue. The eyes are dark brown, the bill is red and the legs and feet are black. The sexes are alike. Resident. Size 40 cms.

White-bellied Go-away-bird
(Corythaixoides leucogast

Found throughout much of the region in dry acacia and riverine woodlands. The head, neck, breast and upperparts are grey, the forehead exhibits a long erectile crest of grey feathers tipped with black. The belly and underparts are white. The wing coverts are grey broadly tipped with black which form bars across the folded wing. The primary wing feathers are black with white at the base. The tail is grey above and black below with a broad white central band. The eyes are dark brown, the bill, legs and feet are blackish. The sexes are alike. Resident. Size 50 cms.

Bare-faced Go-away-bird
(Corythaixoides personate

A bird of thickets, bush and open woodlands, also favouring forests and woodlands with fig trees. The forehead exhibits a long crest of buff-grey feathers, the neck and breast are white, the latter with a flush of green in the centre. The chin and the face to a point to the rear of the eyes is black. The belly is pale buff-grey becoming white on the thighs and undertail coverts. The mantle, back, wings and tail are buff-grey. The eyes are dark brown, the bill, legs and feet are black. The sexes are alike. Resident. Size 50 cms.

Livingstone's Turaco
(Tauraco livingstonir

A reasonably common turaco in the dense forests of southern Tanzania and further south into Malawi and Zimbabwe. The head, neck, mantle and breast are green, the forehead and crown exhibit a long erectile crest of green feathers tipped with white. A white stripe extends from the gape to the apex of the eye and a second stripe runs from below the eye to the ear coverts. A small black patch is present in front of and below the eye. The belly and underparts are blackish. The upperparts and wing coverts are dark green, the primary and secondary wing feathers are bright red tipped with black. The tail is green-blue. The eyes are red-brown, the bill is red and the legs and feet are blackish. The sexes are alike. Resident. Size 40 cms.

Fischer's Turaco
(Tauraco fischeri

A bird with distribution limited in East Africa to forests and woodlands of the coastal regions of Kenya, Tanzania and Somalia. The forehead, face, sides of the neck and the breast are green. The feathers of the forehead, crown and nape form an erectile crest, green at the base with crimson towards the black and white tips, the crimson extends down the hindneck. Two white stripes extend from the gape, one to a point in front of the eye and the second running below the eye to the ear coverts. The eyes are surrounded by a patch of bare red skin. The upperparts are green-blue, the flight feathers are red tipped with black. The eyes are dark brown, the bill red and the legs and feet blackish. The sexes are alike. Resident. Size 40 cms.

Ross's Turaco
(Musophaga rossae)

A bird of savannah woodlands and forests in Uganda, western Kenya and western Tanzania. The overall plumage coloration is glossy blue-black. The forehead and crown have a short erectile crest of crimson. The eyes are surrounded by an area of bright yellow unfeathered skin. The primary and secondary wing feathers are crimson. The eyes are dark brown, the broad bill is bright yellow and the legs and feet are blackish. The sexes are alike. resident. Size 50 cms.

Red-chested Cuckoo
(Cuculus solita:

A cuckoo of woodlands, forests and thickets. The male has the head, mantle and upperparts slaty-grey, chin and throat pale grey and neck and upper breast rufous red. The lower breast and belly are creamy-buff boldly barred with black, the undertail coverts are plain buff-white. The wing coverts are slaty-grey and the primary wing feathers grey with some white barring. The tail is dark grey to black spotted and barred with white. The eyes are dark brown with a yellow orbital ring The bill is black at the tip and yellowish at the base, the legs and feet are bright yellow. The female differs from the male in having a less well developed rufous breast with black barring. Immature birds (illustrated) have head, neck and upperparts black streaked and spotted with white, the nape is white. The breast, belly and underparts are whitish barred with black. The tail is black heavily spotte with white. Resident. Size 30 cms.

Great Spotted Cuckoo
(Clamator glandari:

An inhabitant of dry savannah with sparse trees and bushes. The head is mid-grey with a paler silver-grey crown forming a slight crest. The chin, throat and sides of t neck are creamy-yellow merging to white on the breast, belly and underparts. The hindneck and back are grey-brown, the wings are greyish-brown with scapulars, wing coverts, primaries and secondaries tipped and edged white. The eyes are dark brown with a grey orbital ring, the bill is blackish and the legs and feet are grey. The sexes are alike. Resident and palearctic winter visitor. Size 41 cms.

European Cuckoo
(Cuculus canoru

A palearctic winter visitor throughout the region favouring areas of savannah woodland and forest edges. The male has the head, hindneck, mantle, wing coverts and upperparts slaty-grey. The chin and throat are white with the lower foreneck an upper breast pale grey. The lower breast, belly and underparts are white barred with dark grey. The tail is blackish, spotted, barred and tipped with white. The eyes are yellow, the bill is blackish. The legs and feet are yellow. The sexes are similar but the female has the upper breast barred with grey-black. This species could easily be confused with the African Cuckoo (*Cuculus gularis*) which is paler on the breast, has fainter barring on the flanks and has a yellow base to the bill. Palearctic winter visitor. Size 33 cms.

Didric Cuckoo
(Chrysococcyx caprius

A widespread cuckoo found in a variety of habitats including woodland and forest edges, thornbush country and semi desert areas. The forehead, crown, ear coverts and nape are metallic green. A white eye strip extends from the base of the upper mandible over the eye to the hind-crown and a dark green-black stripe extends from the gape under and to the rear of the eye. The chin, throat and foreneck are white with a dark green moustachial stripe. The breast, belly and underparts are white with a wash of buff on the breast and dark green barring on the flanks. The wing coverts are metallic green, the primary and secondary wing feathers are dark green boldly spotted and barred with white. The eyes are dark red, the bill is blackish and the legs and feet are grey. The sexes are similar, but the female is duller and has white streaking over much of the plumage. Resident. Size 19 cms.

White-browed Coucal
(Centropus supercilliosus)

A common species throughout the region in areas of thickets and tall rank grasses on savannah and in woodland clearings. The feathers of the head, nape and hindneck are earth-brown streaked with white. A prominent white eye stripe extends from the base of the bill along the sides of the crown to the nape. The chin, throat and foreneck are white, the breast, belly and underparts whitish with some barring on the sides of the breast and the flanks. The wings are rich chestnut, the feathers of the mantle and scapulars are chestnut boldly streaked with white-buff. The long tail is blackish-brown narrowly tipped white. The eyes are crimson, the bill black and the legs and feet grey-black. The sexes are alike. Resident. Size 40 cms.

African Marsh Owl

(Asio cape...)

Found in a variety of habitats throughout the region from coastal marshes, savannah grasslands, marshes and mountain moorlands. The facial disc is buff with dark brown patches around the eyes, the remainder of the head, neck and mantle are plain mid-brown, short ear tufts are usually visible. The breast is bro finely barred and flecked with buff. The belly and underparts are plain buff. Th scapulars and wing coverts are mid-brown with buff barring and spotting, the primary and secondary wing feathers and the tail are dark brown with broad bu bars and tips. The eyes are dark brown, the bill is blackish and the legs and feet feathered buff with black claws. The sexes are similar, the females being paler. Resident. Size 36 cms.

Verreaux's Eagle Owl

(Bubo lact...)

A very large owl of thick woodland, riverine forest and wooded savannah throughout the region. The head and face are pale grey-buff with prominent ear tu the facial disc is bordered with a broad black line. The breast, belly and underpart are buff-white with fine dark brown barring on the breast and flanks. The upperpa are grey-brown finely barred with white and dark brown. The scapulars are edged with white which produces a white wing stripe. The primary wing feathers and th tail are dark brown-grey with broad bands of light brown-buff. The eyes are dark brown with pink eyelids, the bill is grey-white, the legs and feet are feathered whit buff with black claws. The sexes are similar, the females being larger than the male Resident. Size 65 cms.

Spotted Eagle Owl

(Bufo african...)

An owl of arid bush, rocky slopes and cliffs, and lightly wooded savannah. The head, breast and underparts are pale buff-white smudged, spotted and finely barre with grey-brown. The facial disc is bordered with a prominent black line and the ea tufts are tipped black. The mantle, back, tail and wing coverts are dark grey-brown finely barred with buff-white. The primary wing feathers are dark brown barred an banded with buff-white. The eyes are yellow (the race *cinerascens* present in northern Kenya and northern Uganda has dark brown eyes). The bill is blackish, the legs and feet are feathered pale buff-white with black claws. The sexes are alike. Resident. Size 50 cms.

Pearl-spotted Owlet

(Glaucidium perlatum

A small owl of savannah and riverine woodlands and dry bush and scrub throughou the region. The head is grey-brown finely spotted with white, the face is white streaked with brown. The throat, breast, belly and underparts are white heavily blotched and streaked with rufous and dark browns. The mantle, back and tail are dark grey-brown with prominent white spots. The scapulars and wing coverts are brown-grey spotted and edged with white, the primary wing feathers are dark brown spotted with buff and white. The eyes are bright yellow, the bill is pale yellow, the legs are feathered white and the feet are pale yellow with grey-black claws. The sexes are alike. Resident. Size 20 cms.

White-faced Scops Owl

(Otus leucotis

A very distinctive owl of woodlands and acacia bush country. The head is mid-grey with fine dark grey-black streaking, the facial disc is white with sparse grey flecking bordered with a broad black line. The ear tufts are mid-grey edged with black. The breast, belly and underparts are pale grey streaked and barred with darker greys. The wings are grey-brown barred and streaked with dark brown, the scapulars have white tips which produces a narrow wing stripe. The tail is grey-brown with dark brown banding. The eyes are golden yellow, the bill is pale yellow and the legs and feet are feathered whitish-buff with black claws. The sexes are alike. Resident. Size 27 cms.

European Nightjar
(Caprimulgus euro

A palearctic winter visitor inhabiting woodlands, thickets and scrub. A nocturr
species that spends the daytime roosting motionless in trees. The head and necl
grey-brown finely streaked and flecked with buff-white and black. A white
moustachial stripe extends from the gape across the lower cheek. The breast, be
and underparts are grey-brown flecked, streaked and barred with dark brown. T
mantle, back and tail are grey-brown finely streaked with black, the latter also
having dark brown barring and white outer tips. The wings are dark brown with
extensive grey and buff barring and spotting, the primaries having some white s
The eyes are dark brown, the small bill is black and the short legs and feet black
The sexes are similar but the female lacks the white on the tail and primaries.
Palearctic winter visitor. Size 27 cms.

Slender-tailed Nightjar
(Caprimulgus c

A resident species throughout Kenya, Uganda and northern Tanzania inhabiting
acacia woodlands and areas of bush and scrub as well as grasslands. The head is
grey-brown with black streaking, a faint rufous brown half collar extends from th
hindneck onto the sides of the neck, and the face is brown with pale flecking. A
narrow buff-white moustachial stripe extends from the gape and a small white p.
is present on the sides of the throat. The breast and underparts are brown-buff wi
black flecking. The wing coverts are grey-brown streaked with black and spotted
with buff. The primary wing feathers are dark brown with white patches. The tai
grey-brown with blackish banding, the central tail feathers are up to 2 cms longer
than the outer feathers. The eyes are dark brown, the short bill and the legs and fe
are blackish. The sexes are similar, the female being duller in appearance. Reside
Size 28 cms.

Alpine Swift
(Tachymarptis me

A large swift which can be seen wheeling around the sky hawking for insects in
central parts of Kenya and northern Tanzania. The head, neck and upper breast ba
are dark brown as are the forked tail, the undertail coverts and the underwings. T
plumage of the upperparts is entirely dark brown. The lower breast and belly are
white and a white patch also usually shows on the chin and throat, but this can be
almost absent in some individuals. The eyes are dark brown, the bill is black and t
short legs and feet pinkish. The sexes are alike. Palearctic winter visitor. Size 22 c

European Swift
(Apus af

Aerial over most habitats including lakes, forests, grasslands, coasts and mountair
The plumage is almost entirely dark brown-black with patches of pale grey on the
forehead, chin and upper throat. The tail is forked. The eyes are dark brown, the b
is black and the legs and feet are grey-black. The sexes are alike. Palearctic winter
visitor. Size 16 cms.

Little Swift
(Apus affir

A common swift of towns and cities, where they breed and roost on buildings ofter
in large congregations. For the most part the plumage is dark brown, the exception
being the very prominent white rump and a white chin and throat patch, there is al
some white flecking on the head and face. The end of the tail is square not forked.
The eyes are dark brown, the bill, legs and feet are blackish. The sexes are alike.
Resident. Size 13 cms.

Palm Swift
(Cypsiurus parv

A very thin narrow swift with long wings and a deeply forked tail, encountered
hawking for insects over arid bush, woodlands and towns. The plumage on the
upperparts is olive-brown with darker brown primary and secondary wing feathers
The underparts are grey-brown slightly paler on the chin and throat. The eyes are
dark brown, the bill, legs and feet are blackish. The sexes are alike. Resident.
Size 13 cms.

Speckled Mousebird
(Colius str

A common species over much of the region found in a wide range of habitats fro woodlands, areas of bush and scrub, parks, gardens, towns and cultivated farml The forehead,face and chin are black, the crown with it's short crest, and the hindneck are grey-brown, the ear coverts are white. The throat and foreneck are brown flecked with black, the breast, belly and underparts are buff-brown with darker brown barring on the breast. The mantle, back and wing coverts are grey-brown, the primary wing feathers are darkish brown. The tail is grey-brown the central feathers being very long, the outer feathers are edged white. The eyes are brown, the bill is greyish-black, the legs and feet are red. The sexes are alike. The are usually encountered in small family flocks foraging among vegetation for fru buds and other plant matter. Easily recognised in flight with the long tail and sho wings which beat rapidly between short intervals of gliding. Resident.Size 33 cm

White-headed Mousebird
(Colius leucoceph

A bird of dry areas restricted in distribution to north, east and south-eastern Ken southern Somalia and north-eastern Tanzania. The forehead, crown, crest and na are white, the ear coverts and upper cheeks are greyish-white surrounding a dark patch. The throat, neck, mantle, back and wing coverts are buff grey-white boldly barred with black. The breast, belly and underparts are buff. The primary and secondary wing feathers are grey-buff. The very long tail is grey above and grey-brown below. The uppertail coverts are grey with fine black barring. The eyes are dark brown, the bill is blue-grey at the base and black at the tip, the legs and feet a red. The sexes are alike. Resident. Size 31 cms.

Blue-naped Mousebird
(Urocolius macrou

Normally encountered in small flocks inhabiting areas of bush and scrub, thicket and vegetation along rivers and streams. The forehead, crown, crest and face are grey, the nape is bright turquoise blue. An area of bright red unfeathered skin surrounds the eyes. The mantle, back and neck are grey-brown, the breast is grey merging to buff on the belly and underparts. The wing coverts are grey-brown and the primary and secondary wing feathers are dark brown edged with grey and buf The extremely long tail is bluish-grey darkening towards the tip. The eyes are red, the bill is black with the base of the upper mandible red. The legs and feet are pinkish-red. The sexes are alike. Immature birds lack the turquoise blue nape and have a greenish-grey bill. They are usually encountered in small flocks of 4-6 individuals feeding on fruits and leaves. Resident. Size 36 cms.

Giant Kingfisher
(Megaceryle maxin

The largest of Africa's kingfishers well distributed in southern Kenya, Uganda an Tanzania always in the vicinity of water, favouring the wooded banks of streams and rivers, lakes and ponds. Often well concealed in overhanging foliage from where they plunge-dive for fish, crabs and amphibians. The male has the forehead crown and nape black spotted with white, the feathers being loosely arranged to form a spiky crest. The chin, throat and lower cheeks are white broken by a narro black moustachial stripe. The breast is a rich chestnut, the belly and underparts a white boldly spotted with black. The wings and tail are black boldly spotted and barred with white. The eyes are dark brown, the bill greyish-black and the legs an feet are grey-brown. The female (illustrated) differs from the male in having the breast white, boldly spotted with black and the belly and underparts rich chestnu Resident. Size 42 cms.

Pied Kingfisher
(Ceryle

Widely distributed throughout the region in the vicinity of water. The only all b
and white kingfisher in East Africa. The forehead, crown, nape and hindneck ar
black. A white stripe extends from the upper mandible above the eye to the nap
a black stripe extends from the gape through and below the eye to the black ear
coverts. The chin, throat and foreneck are white, the breast, belly and underpart
white with two black bands extending across the breast of the male, while in the
female there is a single band which fails to join at the centre of the breast. The w
back and tail are black irregularly spotted and barred with white. The eyes are d
brown, the bill, legs and feet are black. Resident. Size 25 cms.

Malachite Kingfisher
(Corythornis cri

One of East Africa's most colourful birds, found along rivers and streams, coasta
estuaries and mangroves. The forehead, crown and nape are iridescent greenish-
barred with black. The chin, throat and centre of the breast are white merging w
bright rufous cheeks, sides of breast and underparts. A white patch is present at
base of the ear coverts. The mantle and tail are dark blue, the back and rump are
iridescent azure blue. The scapulars and wing coverts are dark blue spotted with
azure, the primary wing feathers are dark blue-black. The eyes are dark brown, th
bill, legs and feet are bright red. The sexes are alike. Resident. Size 14 cms.

Pygmy Kingfisher
(Ceyx p

One of the smallest of Africa's kingfishers, found in woodlands, river side forests
along rivers and streams and in areas of lush tall grasses. The forehead and crown
dark blue barred with black, the hindneck, sides of neck, cheeks and face are orar
with a flush of violet in the region of the ear coverts, below which is a prominent
white patch. The chin and throat are white, the breast, belly and underparts are
orange. The mantle, scapulars and rump are dark iridescent blue, the primary anc
secondary wing feathers and the tail are blackish. The eyes are dark brown, the bi
legs and feet are orange-red. The sexes are alike. Resident. Size 11 cms.

Woodland Kingfisher
(Halcyon senegale

A bird of wooded savannah, parks and gardens. The forehead, crown, nape and
hindneck are greyish-white with a flush of blue. A black patch extends from the b
of the upper mandible to encircle the eye. The chin and throat are white, the sides
the neck and breast are pale grey, the belly and underparts are white with a wash c
grey-blue on the flanks. The scapulars, back, rump and upper tail are bright azure
blue. The wing coverts are black, the primary wing feathers are azure broadly edge
with black, the secondaries are azure tipped with black. The eyes are dark brown,
the bill is unusual in having the upper mandible bright red and the lower mandibl
black. The legs and feet are blackish. The sexes are alike. Resident. Size 20 cms.

Striped Kingfisher
(Halcyon chelic

Found in areas of light woodland and isolated groups of trees on grasslands and
savannah. The forehead, crown and nape are brown-black finely streaked with gre
white. A black stripe extends from the base of the bill through the eye to the sides c
the nape. The hindneck and sides of the neck are grey-white with sparse dark brow
speckling. The chin, throat, breast, belly and underparts are white, the breast havir
a wash of buff and being lightly streaked with brown, the flanks are heavily streake
with brown. The wing coverts are dark brown-black edged with white, the primary
wing feathers are dark brown and the secondaries are brown broadly edged with
azure blue. The back and rump are azure blue and the tail is grey-blue. The eyes are
dark brown, the bill is blackish the lower mandible being red towards the base. The
legs and feet are dull pink-red. The sexes are alike. Resident. Size 16 cms.

Grey-headed Kingfisher
(Halcyon leucocepha

Found in woodlands, riverine forests and lightly wooded savannah. The head, nec
chin, throat and breast bib are greyish-white, the sides of the breast, the belly and
underparts are rich chestnut. The scapulars and wing coverts are black, the primary
wing feathers are black broadly edged with bright azure blue. The back, rump and
tail are azure blue. The eyes are dark brown, the bill, legs and feet are bright red. Th
sexes are alike. Resident. Size 20 cms.

Madagascar Bee-eater
(Merops supercili

Found over much of the region. The forehead and eyebrow are white. The crown olive green. A black stripe bordered below with white, extends from the gape through the eye to the sides of the nape. The chin is pale yellow becoming orange red on the throat. The breast, belly and underparts are leaf green. The mantle and back are green, the wing coverts olive green and the primary wing feathers are gre edged with brown. The eyes are deep red, the bill is black and the legs and feet are greyish-black. The sexes are alike. Resident. Size 29 cms.

Blue-cheeked Bee-eater
(Merops persi

A winter visitor to East Africa usually found close to water where they frequent papyrus reedbeds and lake side trees. The forehead is white with a faint wash of blue. The crown, nape, back and long tail are leaf green. A broad black stripe exten from the gape through the eye to the ear coverts and is bordered above and , to a lesser extent, below with pale blue. The cheeks are pale blue-white. The chin is pa yellow graduating to orange-red on the throat. The breast, belly and underparts are yellowish-green. The wings are leaf green, the primaries being edged with dark brown-black. The eyes are deep red, the bill is black and the legs and feet are brow black. The sexes are alike. Palearctic winter visitor. Size 30 cms.

European Bee-eater
(Merops apiast

A palearctic winter visitor and passage migrant found over a wide range of habitats including woodlands, cultivated farmland, wooded savannah, lakes and rivers. Th forehead is white, the crown, nape and mantle are chestnut. A black patch extends from the gape and covers the eye and ear coverts bordered below with white, becoming yellow on the chin and throat. A narrow black band separates the throat from the blue-green breast, belly and underparts. The scapulars, back and rump are golden yellow. The wing coverts are green and chestnut, the primaries are blue-gree tipped black. The tail is green. The eyes are rich red, the bill is black and the legs an feet are blackish-brown. The sexes are similar, the female being duller above and paler below. Palearctic winter visitor. Size 28 cms.

Carmine Bee-eater
(Merops nubicu

A species easily recognised by the bright carmine red plumage. The forehead, crow chin and throat are iridescent blue-green, a black band extends from the gape to the ear coverts. The nape, neck, breast and belly are bright reddish-pink, the undertail coverts are pale blue-green. The mantle and scapulars are reddish-pink. The wings and tail are carmine red, the tertials are edged blue, the primaries and secondaries are edged and tipped black, and the long central tail feathers darken towards the tip. The uppertail coverts are blue-green. The eyes are dark red, the bill, legs and feet are black. The sexes are alike. Resident. Size 37 cms.

White-throated Bee-eater
(Merops albicollis

A species encountered in a range of habitats. The forehead is white extending as a stripe around the head to the nape, the crown is black. A black stripe extends from the gape through the eye to the ear coverts. The chin, throat and cheeks are white. A broad black band extends across the upper breast bordered below with a band of pale blue, becoming pale green on the lower breast. The belly and underparts are white. The nape is orange-buff merging into green on the mantle and back. The wing coverts are green-blue, the primaries and secondaries are bluish, the tail is green-blue with very long blackish central streamers. The eyes are dark red, the bill is black, the legs and feet are greyish. The sexes are similar. Resident. Size 28 cms.

Cinnamon-chested Bee-eater
(Merops oreobates

A bird of woodland edges and clearings. The forehead, crown. nape, back, mantle and wing coverts are bright green. A black stripe extends from the gape to the ear coverts. The chin and throat are yellow and a broad black band extends across the upper breast. The lower breast is rich cinnamon red merging to yellow-buff on the belly and underparts. The primary and secondary wing feathers are green edged with black. The tail is square, bright green above with a black band towards the tip. The eyes are dark red, the bill, legs and feet are blackish. The sexes are alike. Immature birds (illustrated) lack the black breast band and have finely streaked underparts. Resident. Size 22 cms.

Little Bee-eater
(Merops pusi...

The most widely distributed East African bee-eaters. The forehead, crown and upperparts are rich leaf green. A black stripe extends from the gape through the ey... to the ear coverts. The eyebrow line is metallic ultramarine blue. The chin and th... are pale yellow, a black band is present in the centre of the upper breast, the remainder of the breast being rich orange-red becoming paler on the belly and underparts. The wings are green the primary wing feathers being edged with olive and the secondaries with rufous-black. The central tail feathers are green the outer feathers rufous tipped black, the tail is slightly forked. The eyes are red, the bill, le... and feet blackish. The sexes are alike. Resident. Size 15 cms.

Somali Bee-eater
(Merops revo...

Found in arid areas of thornbush and scrub, coastal dunes and cultivated farmland... The feathers of the forehead and crown are pale olive green and have a spiky appearance. A black stripe runs from the gape through and beyond the eye above which is a bright blue eyebrow stripe. The chin and throat are white, the breast and belly are buff and the undertail coverts are pale blue. The nape is buff blending wit... the green mantle and back. The wings are green the primaries and secondaries edge... with brown. The tail is blue-green. The eyes are red, the bill is black and the legs an... feet are greyish. The sexes are alike. Resident. Size 16 cms.

White-fronted Bee-eater
(Merops bullockoid...

This species is mainly restricted to the Rift Valley in Kenya and to southern Tanzania. The forehead is white becoming buff to pale orange on the crown and nape. A black stripe extends from the base of the bill through the eye to the ear coverts below which is a white band from the ear coverts to the chin. The throat is bright scarlet red. The breast and belly are orange-buff, the undertail coverts blue. The upperparts including the wings and tail are green-blue. The eyes are brown, the... bill, legs and feet are blackish. The sexes are alike. Resident. Size 23 cms.

Lilac-breasted Roller
(Coracias caudat...

The commonest of East Africa's rollers found in woodland, open thornbush country and lightly wooded savannah. The forehead and eyebrow are white, the crown and nape are pale green. A narrow black stripe runs through the eye, the cheeks are rufous with a wash of lilac. The chin is white, the throat and breast are lilac streaked with white. The belly and underparts are turquoise blue. The mantle, back and scapulars are brown, the rump is dark blue with turquoise blue uppertail coverts. The tail is azure blue with long central streamers darkish blue and brown. The wing coverts are dark and azure blue, the primaries are bright azure blue and black. The eyes are dark brown, the bill is blackish and the legs and feet yellowish-pink. The sexes are alike. Resident. Size 40 cms.

European Roller
(Coracias garrulus

A winter visitor throughout the region. The head, neck, breast, belly and underparts are pale turquoise blue, whitish on the forehead and cheeks. There is a narrow black stripe through the eye. The mantle, back and scapulars are rufous brown, the rump and uppertail coverts are dark green-blue. The tail is azure blue with darker blue central feathers. The wing coverts are dark blue to bright azure, the primaries are blue-black. The eyes are dark brown, the bill is black and the legs and feet are dull yellow-pink. The sexes are alike. Palearctic winter visitor. Size 30 cms.

Rufous-crowned Roller
(Coracias naevia)

An inhabitant of dry woodlands and lightly wooded savannah. The forehead and eyebrow are white, the crown, nape and hindneck are dull cinnamon-brown, the latter having a central white patch. The chin is white, the cheeks, throat, breast and belly are dark lilac heavily streaked with white. The mantle and scapulars are olive brown with a flush of green, the back is lilac blending to dark purple-blue on the rump and uppertail coverts. The tail is purple-blue with the central tail feathers olive brown. The wing coverts are dark purple at the carpal joint blending into lilac and rufous brown on the greater coverts, the primaries are dark blue edged with blue-green. The eyes are dark brown, the bill is blackish and the legs and feet are dull ochre. The sexes are alike. Resident. Size 33 cms.

African Hoopoe
(Upupa epops africa

A bird of wooded savannah, cultivated land, pastures and short grassy areas in pa
and gardens. Difficult to confuse with any other species. The head, neck, mantle,
breast and belly are bright rufous, the undertail coverts are buff-white. The feather
of the forehead and crown form a crest which, when erect, is fan-shaped, these
feathers are tipped with black. The wings are black with broad white bands, the
primary and secondary feathers are black with a white band towards the tips. The
tail is black with a broad white band across the centre. The eyes are dark brown, th
long decurved bill is blackish and the legs and feet are grey-black. The sexes are
similar, the female being duller and slightly smaller. Resident. Size 28 cms.

Green Wood Hoopoe
(Phoeniculus purpure

A species found in most types of woodland, usually encountered in noisy flocks
foraging from tree to tree in search of insects. A slender bird with the bulk of the
plumage dark green-blue with an iridescent sheen showing purple and violet. The
primary coverts and wing feathers have white bars which are very prominent in
flight, as are the white spots that are present towards the end of the very long tail.
The eyes are dark brown, the decurved bill and the legs and feet are bright red. The
sexes are similar, the female being slightly smaller. Resident. Size 40 cms.

African Scimitarbill
(Phoeniculus cyanomela

Found over much of the region in woodlands, dry thorn bush areas and in lightly
wooded savannah. The entire plumage is dark iridescent blue-black with washes o
violet on the throat, breast and rump. The primary wing feathers and the very long
tail have some prominent white spots. The eyes are dark brown, the very long
decurved bill and the legs and feet are black. The female shows brown-black on the
throat and breast and the primaries are faintly tipped greyish. Usually encountered
in small groups of about 6 birds foraging on the trunks and branches of trees in
search of a wide variety of insect foods. Resident. Size 28 cms.

White-headed Barbet
(Lybius leucocephalu

A species found throughout Uganda, central and southern Kenya and northern
Tanzania, inhabiting woodlands, favouring areas with fig trees, cultivated farmland
and parks and gardens. The head, mantle, neck, breast and rump are white. The bell
is brownish-black streaked with white and the undertail coverts are white. The back
is brownish-black, the wing coverts are black with white spots and the primary wing
feathers are black finely edged with white. The tail is black-brown. The eyes are dar
brown, the heavy bill and the legs and feet are blackish-grey. The sexes are alike.
Resident. Size 16 cms.

Red & Yellow Barbet
(Trachyphonus erythrocephalus

A species that favours dry bush country, lightly wooded savannah and scrub areas
usually in the vicinity of termite mounds in which they breed. The male has the
forehead and crown black and the nape red and yellow spotted with black. The chin
and the centre of the throat are black, the sides of the throat are yellow and the
cheeks are red. The breast, belly and underparts are yellow, the former with a
necklace of black feathers spotted with white. The back is black spotted with white
and yellow, the rump is yellow and the uppertail coverts are red tipped with yellow.
The tail is black heavily barred with yellow-white. The wing feathers are blackish
boldly spotted with white. The eyes are brown, the bill is orange-red darker at the
tip, the legs and feet are dark grey. The female lacks the black throat patch and the
black crown, and is generally not so bright as the male. Resident. size 23 cms.

D'Arnaud's Barbet
(Trachyphonus darnaundii)

A species that favours areas of arid bush, open woodlands, acacia scrub and lightly
wooded grasslands. The head, neck and throat are yellow heavily speckled with
dark brown-black, the breast is yellow with an irregular black patch in the centre and
with fine black flecking. The belly is pale yellow-white, the undertail coverts are
white tipped with bright red. The mantle, back, wings and tail are black-brown
boldly spotted and barred with yellow and white. The eyes are brown, the bill, legs
and feet are blackish. The sexes are alike. Resident. Size 16 cms.

Grey Hornbill

(Tockus nas...

A species of open woodlands and lightly wooded savannah. The head and neck a... dark grey with a white stripe extending from just above the eye, along the edge of ... crown and down the hindneck. The breast is buff-brown fading to white on the be... and underparts. The mantle and back are brown, the latter with a white central stripe. The tail is dark brown tipped white. The wing coverts and primaries are da... brown edged with buff and white. The eyes are dark brown, the large decurved bi... blackish with a white stripe along the lower side of the upper mandible, the legs a... feet are black-brown. The female differs from the male in having the upper mandi... creamy-yellow at the base and red at the tip. A small patch of bare skin on the thro... is pale yellow-green. Resident. Size 48 cms.

Red-billed Hornbill

(Tockus enythrorhync...

A common species in arid bush regions and in open woodlands. The forehead, crown and nape are black, the remainder of the head and neck are white with grey smudges on the ear coverts and the sides of the neck. The breast, belly and underparts are white. The mantle and back are black-brown with a white central stripe, the long tail is black the outer feathers with white. The wing coverts and primaries are black with bold white spots. The eyes are dark brown, the decurved bill is red with the basal, section of the lower mandible blackish. The legs and feet are blackish-brown. The female is smaller than the male and has less black on the bill. Resident. Size 45 cms.

Von Der Decken's Hornbill

(Tockus decke...

A bird of bush areas and acacia woodlands. The crown and nape are black, the rest of the head, neck, breast and underparts are white. A black patch surrounds the eye and the ear coverts are streaked with grey-black, the sides of the throat have patche... of bare pink-red skin. The back is black with a white central stripe, the rump and ta... are black with the outer tail feathers showing much white from midway to the tips. The wing coverts and primaries are black, the secondaries are white. The eyes are dark brown, the large decurved bill is red at the base and dull yellow towards the ti... The legs and feet are black. The female has an all black bill and is smaller than the male. Resident. Size 49 cms.

Yellow-billed Hornbill

(Tockus flavirostr...

A bird of arid bush country and lightly wooded savannah. The forehead, crown and nape are black, the head and neck are white with a black patch around the eye and black streaking on the ear coverts and the sides of the neck. The throat has a patch o... bare pink skin, the breast, belly and underparts are white. The black back has a broa... white central stripe, the rump and tail are black the outer tail feathers with white tip... and a broad white midway band. The wing coverts and primaries are black spotted with white. The eyes are yellow, the large decurved bill is yellow and the legs and feet are black-brown. Resident. Size 50 cms.

Silvery-cheeked Hornbill

(Ceratogymna brevi...

A large hornbill of mountain and coastal forests. The plumage is mainly black, the belly and underparts are white, along with the rump and uppertail coverts, the tail i... tipped white and the cheeks are streaked with grey. The eyes are dark brown with a blue orbital ring, the enormous bill has a yellow band at the base, is brownish-black with a large creamy-yellow casque. the legs and feet are black. The female is smaller than the male and the bill casque is much reduced. Resident. Size 70 cms.

Ground Hornbill

(Bucorvus cafer...

A very large bird, spending most of the day on the ground in search of food which consists of snakes, amphibians, rodents and a variety of insects. The plumage is almost entirely black, the exception being the white primary wing feathers. A patch of bright red unfeathered skin surrounds the eyes and extends on to the sides of the neck and the throat. The eyes are yellow, the large decurved bill is black with a short casque at the upper base. The legs and feet are black. The female is smaller than the male and has a throat patch of blue-grey and red. Immature birds have brown-black plumage, primaries streaked with black, pale yellow-grey eyes and facial and throat patch greyish-yellow. Resident. size 107 cms.

Nubian Woodpecker

(Campethera nub[...]

A bird of open woodlands and bush. The male has the forehead, crown and nape r[...] the remainder of the head and neck are white with blackish flecks and streaks. Th[...] chin is white and the moustachial stripe is red bordered with black. The breast, be[...] and underparts are creamy white with black spots on the breast and undertail coverts and black barring on the flanks. The scapulars and wing coverts are green-brown barred with creamy-yellow. The back, rump and uppertail coverts are greenish-brown barred and spotted with white. The tail is greenish barred with brown. The primary wing feathers are brown barred with white. The eyes are dark red, the bill, legs and feet are greyish-black. The female has the forehead and crow[...] black, spotted with white and the moustachial stripe is black finely flecked with white. Resident. Size 18 cms.

Golden-tailed Woodpecker

(Campethera abingo[...]

An inhabitant of various woodland types, thickets and bushes. The male has the forehead, crown and nape red with grey-black streaking and flecking, particularly the forehead and forecrown. The sides of the head and neck are white heavily spotted with black, the eyebrow is white. The moustachial stripe is red. The chin and throat are white with much black spotting, the breast, belly and underparts are creamy-yellow with heavy black streaks on the breast and some black spotting on t[...] belly. The upperparts are olive-green with yellowish bars, the tail is olive brown with yellowish bars and bright yellow shafts. The eyes are dark red, the bill, legs an[...] feet are dark grey. The female has the forehead and moustachial stripe black-brown[...] finely spotted white. Resident. Size 18 cms.

Cardinal Woodpecker

(Denropicos fuscescer[...]

Found throughout the region in areas of arid bush and most types of woodland and[...] forest. The forehead and forecrown are buff-brown, the hindcrown and the nape ar[...] red. The sides of the head are white finely flecked and streaked with grey-brown. A[...] black moustachial stripe extends from the base of the bill to the lower neck. The chin, throat and breast are white boldly marked with brown-black streaks. The bell[...] and underparts are creamy-white streaked and barred with brown-black. The upperparts are dark brown barred with white, the uppertail coverts are tipped with red. The eyes are reddish-brown, the bill, legs and feet are blackish. The female differs from the male in having black-brown nape and crown. Immature birds are a duller version of the adults and have a red crown patch. Resident. Size 13 cms.

Grey Woodpecker

(Dendropicos goerta[...]

A bird of woodland and forest edges and acacia woodlands and clearings, often foraging on the ground. The forehead, cheeks and ear coverts are grey, the crown an[...] nape are red edged with white. The neck, chin, throat and breast are grey and the underparts are greyish with a tinge of yellow. A patch of yellow-orange appears on the belly and some grey barring on the flanks. The back and wing coverts are yellowish-green, the primary and secondary wing feathers are dark brown edged with green and barred with white. The rump and uppertail coverts are red. The tail i[...] dark brown barred with white. The eyes are darkish brown, the bill is black and the legs and feet are greyish. The female lacks the red crown and nape of the male, the head being all grey. Resident. Size 18 cms.

Bearded Woodpecker

(Dendropicos namaquus[...]

A large woodpecker found in acacia woodlands and forests. The forehead and forecrown are black finely spotted with white. The hindcrown is red, the hindneck black. The sides of the neck and head are white with a patch of black extending from the rear of the eye and covering the ear coverts. Another patch of black extends from the base of the bill broadening onto the sides of the neck. The chin and throat are white. The breast, belly and underparts are greyish barred with creamy-white. The back and wings are brown barred with white, the primary wing feathers being edged with yellowish-green. The eyes are red-brown, the bill, legs and feet are greyish-black. The female differs form the male in having the crown black not red. Resident. Size 23 cms.

Rufous-naped Lark
(Mirafra afric

A common resident species on open plains and in bushy terrain throughout much of the region. The feathers of the forehead and crown are greyish brown streaked with black, the nape feathers are usually rufous but there is a certain amount of regional variation. The face, chin and throat are buff-white, the cheeks and ear coverts are mid-brown. The breast, belly and underparts are buff with a wash of rufous on the upper breast and flanks. The breast is spotted with dark brown. The wings are rounded, dark brown with streaks of rufous and black. The back, rump and tail feathers are dark brown streaked with black and edged with buff. The eyes and bill are brown, the legs and feet are flesh pink. The sexes are alike. Resident. Size 17 cm

Red-winged Bush Lark
(Mirafra hyperme

Found throughout most of the region in areas of open grassy plains interspersed with bushes. They can usually be located singing from the tops of low bushes and shrub the song consisting of a short series of clear repeated whistles. They can be distinguished from the Rufous-naped Lark by their larger size and longer tail. The forehead, crown, nape and mantle are greyish brown, boldly streaked with black. The face is buff-white with some irregular speckling, a pale stripe extends above the eye from the forehead to the hind-crown. The chin and throat are white, the breast buff. The sides of the neck and the breast are heavily spotted with dark brown and black. The primary and secondary flight feathers are rufous edged and tipped with brown and buff. The rump and tail are brown edged with grey and buff. The eyes are brown, the bill is dark brown/black, paler at the base, and the legs and feet are grey/pink. The sexes are alike. Resident. Size 23 cms.

Crested Lark
(Galerida crista

A locally common species in northern Kenya and southern Ethiopia. The forehead and crown are pale buff streaked with brown/black, the feathering of the crown forming an erectile crest. The nape, mantle and sides of the neck are buff streaked and speckled with mid-brown. The chin, throat and breast are buff, heavily streaked with dark brown, the belly and underparts are whitish with a wash of buff on the flanks. The back, wing coverts and flight feathers are brown edged with buff. The tail is dark brown and rufous, paler on the outer edges. The eyes are deep brown. The bill is dark brown/black, paler at the base. The legs and feet are flesh coloured. The sexes are alike. Resident and partial migrant. Size 16 cms.

Red-capped Lark
(Calandrella cinere

A bird favouring areas of short dry grassland. A medium-sized, slender lark with forehead and erectile crest feathers rufous. The nape, mantle, cheeks and sides of the neck are brown/buff. A pronounced white stripe extends from above the eye to the hind-crown. The chin and throat are white, the breast is brownish buff with prominent rufous patches on the sides, the belly and underparts are white. The back is brown merging to rufous on the rump and becoming dark brown on the tail, the outer edges of which are whitish-buff. The wing coverts and flight feathers are dark brown edged and tipped with pale brown and buff. The eyes are dark brown, the bill is black and the legs and feet are brownish-black. The sexes are alike. Resident. Size 14 cms.

Fischer's Sparrow Lark
(Eremopterix leucopareia

A small rather finch-like lark of south-western Kenya, north, central and western Tanzania and north-eastern Uganda. The adult male has the forehead, crown, nape and neck chestnut brown. The face is black with one black stripe extending from the eye to the hind-crown and another extending from the chin, down the throat and around the sides of the neck and running down the centre of the breast, belly and underparts. The cheeks and ear coverts are creamy white. The sides of the breast, the belly and the flanks are white with a wash of buff. The wing coverts and flight feathers are dark brown, broadly edged with grey, buff and rufous. The tail is dark brown edged with grey and rufous. The female lacks the bold markings of the male having a grey-brown head streaked with dark brown and a hint of rufous brown around the neck. the breast is buff and a broad central band of brown extends down the centre of the white belly and underparts. The eyes are brown, the thickish bill greyish blue-black and the legs and feet brown. Resident. Size 11 cms.

Banded Martin
(Riparia cin...)

Found in areas of open grassland and bush, often in small parties. The plumage of the upper side of the body, from the forehead to the tail is a uniform dark chocolate brown. A short narrow stripe extends from the base of the upper mandible to the eyebrow. The chin, throat and sides of the neck are buff-white, a broad chocolate brown band extends across the upper breast, while the lower breast, belly and underparts are white. In flight the primary and secondary wing feathers appear slightly darker than the rest of the upper plumage and contrast strongly with the white under wing coverts. The tail is unforked. The eyes, legs and feet are dark brown and the bill is black. The sexes are alike. Resident. Size 16 cms.

African Rock Martin
(Hirundo fuligu...)

A widely distributed species around kopjes, cliffs, mountains, rocky hill sides and human habitations. The plumage is almost entirely dark brown, slightly darker above than below, occasionally with a faint wash of grey on the wings and tail. The chin and throat are pale rufous. The unforked tail has a series of white spots toward the tip which are only visible when the tail is spread in flight. The eyes are dark brown, the bill is black and the legs and feet are greyish-brown. The sexes are alike. Resident. Size 13 cms.

Wire-tailed Swallow
(Hirundo smith...)

A common species throughout the region on savannahs, along rivers, and around lakes and human habitations. The forehead and crown are bright rufous, the face, nape, mantle, back and wing coverts are glossy, dark violet blue. The chin, throat, breast, belly and underparts are white, a violet blue patch extends from the sides of the neck to the sides of the breast and a similar patch extends from the rear of the flanks around the sides onto the undertail coverts. The primary and secondary flight feathers are purple-black above and whitish-grey below. The rump and tail are purple-black, the outermost tail feathers forming into long thin wire-like streamers. The eyes are dark brown, the bill, legs and feet are black. The sexes are similar, the female having less well developed tail streamers. Resident. Size 15 cms.

Mosque Swallow
(Hirundo senegalensis...)

The largest swallow in East Africa. An inhabitant of open country, light woodlands, river edges and coastal bush over much of the region. The forehead, crown, nape, mantle, back, wings and tail are deep blue-black. The cheeks, ear coverts, rump, belly and underparts are rufous, the chin, throat and breast are whitish merging into the rufous feathering of the belly. The underwing coverts are whitish and the underside of the flight feathers are greyish. The outermost tail feathers are elongated, resulting in a deeply forked tail, particularly noticeable in flight. The eyes are dark brown, the bill, legs and feet are black. The sexes are alike. Resident. Size 23 cms.

Red-rumped Swallow
(Hirundo daurica)

A bird of open grasslands, rocky hill sides and human habitations. The upper plumage resembles that of the Mosque Swallow, with forehead, crown, nape, back and wing coverts dark, glossy blue-black. The sides of the neck and the rump are rufous. The chin, throat, breast, belly and underparts are off-white with faint streaks of dark grey. The primary and secondary wing feathers are dark blue-black. The tail is blue-black and deeply forked. The eyes are dark brown, the bill is black and the legs and feet are brownish-black. The sexes are alike. Resident and winter migrant. Size 18 cms.

Striped Swallow
(Hirundo abyssinica)

A common and well distributed species throughout the region, inhabiting areas of open grassland, cultivated farmland, human habitations and woodland edges. One of the prettiest of East Africa's swallows, with the forehead, crown, nape, sides of the neck and rump rusty red. The chin, throat, cheeks, breast, belly and underparts are white boldly streaked with black. The flight feathers are black with a wash of brown. The tail is bluish-black and deeply forked. The eyes are dark brown, the bill, legs and feet are black. The sexes are similar, the female having shorter outer tail feathers. Resident. Size 18 cms.

African Pied Wagtail
(Motacilla agu...

A common species over most of the region. The forehead, crown, nape, back, win... coverts and cheeks are black. A broad black band extends across the upper breast the chin, throat, lower breast, belly and underparts are white. The primary wing feathers are black edged and tipped with white. The central tail feathers are black and the outer feathers white. The eyes are dark brown, the bill is black and the leg and feet dark grey-black. The sexes are similar. Resident. Size 20 cms.

Yellow Wagtail
(Motacilla fla...

A widely distributed and common species throughout the region. Several races of yellow wagtail occur during periods of migration, when they exhibit great variatic in head plumage from white to yellow, grey, blue and black. In most races the remainder of the plumage is similar. The throat, breast, belly and underparts are bright yellow. The back and wing coverts are olive green and the primary and secondary wing feathers are black edged with whitish-buff. The tail is brown-blac with the outermost feathers white. The eyes are dark brown, the bill, legs and feet a black. Winter visitor and passage migrant. Size 16 cms.

Richard's Pipit
(Anthus novaeseelandi...

A common and widely distributed species, found in areas of open grasslands and savannahs. The plumage of the upperparts is buff-brown with dark streaking. A broad off-white stripe follows the line of the eyebrow and the chin, throat, cheeks and ear coverts are off-white with some buff streaking. The narrow eye and moustachial stripes are dark brown. The breast, belly and underparts are buffish with some dark streaking on the upper breast. The wing feathers are brown edged with buff, The tail is darkish-brown, the outermost feathers being edged with white The eyes are dark brown, the bill is black with some yellowish-brown at the base an the legs and feet are warm brown. The sexes are alike. Resident. Size 15 cms.

Golden Pipit
(Tmetothylacus tenellu...

A bird of the dry bush and scrub areas. The male in flight is unmistakeable, appearing as a burst of brilliant chrome yellow. The forehead, crown, nape, mantle and ear coverts are olive green streaked with black. The face, chin, throat, breast and underparts are brilliant chrome yellow. A broad black band extends across the breast. The wing coverts are yellow edged with dark brown, the secondary wing feathers are yellow and the primary wing feathers yellow edged and tipped with black. The central tail feathers are dark brown while the outer feathers are bright yellow. The eyes and bill are dark brown, the legs and feet are pale flesh pink. The female lacks much of the brilliant yellow found in the male, she also lacks the black breast band. Resident. Size 15 cms.

Yellow-throated Longclaw
(Macronyx croceus,

A reasonably common bird in grassland and savannah regions. The forehead, crown and nape are mid-brown streaked with dark brown. A band of yellow follows the line of the eyebrow and the chin, throat, lower breast, and underparts are the same bright yellow. A narrow black moustachial stripe extends down the sides of the neck, joining a broad black breast band, some black spotting occurs on the breast below this band. The wing coverts are brown edged with buff and the primary and secondary wing feathers are brown edged with yellow and buff. The tail is dark brown tipped with white. The eyes and bill are dark brown, the legs and feet are dull yellow-pink. The female has a duller appearance than the male. Resident. Size 20 cms.

Rosy-breasted Longclaw *(Macronyx ameliae)*

A bird of moist grasslands, floodplains and the margins of open water. The forehead, crown, nape, mantle and wing coverts are warm brown streaked with dark brown-black. The face is buff-white with a brown eye stripe thickening at the rear to cover the ear coverts. A narrow black moustachial stripe extends down the sides of the neck before linking with a broad black breast band. The chin and throat are bright rosy-red, the lower breast and upper belly are washed pink and the remainder of the underparts are buff-white. The primary and secondary wing feathers are warm brown edged with buff. The tail is dark brown tipped and edged with white. Resident. Size 18 cms.

Yellow-vented Bulbul
(Pycnonotus barba

Probably the commonest bird in East Africa, being found throughout the region is
wide variety of habitats. The head, face and chin are black, becoming dark brown
the throat, breast, ear coverts and the slightly crested nape. The belly and flanks a
off-white and the feathers of the undertail are bright yellow. The upperparts
including the wing coverts are grey-brown. The primary and secondary wing
feathers are darkish grey-brown edged with buff. The tail is dark brown with a
variable amount of white at the tip. There are several races found within the regio
some of which show white on the sides of the neck and ear coverts, the yellow on
undertail coverts is also variable or absent. The eyes are dark brown, the bill, legs
and feet are black. The sexes are alike. Resident. Size 18 cms.

White-crowned Shrike
(Eurocephalus ruppe

A bird of dry thornbush country, locally common throughout the region. The
forehead and crown are white, a black band extends from the base of the bill throu
the eye before broadening to cover the ear coverts and the nape. The chin, throat,
breast, belly and underparts are white, a brown patch is visible on the sides of the
breast. The mantle and wing coverts are greyish-brown, the primary and secondar
flight feathers are dark brown. The rump is white and very conspicuous in flight, t
tail is dark brown. The eyes, which have a narrow orbital ring of white, are dark
brown, the bill, legs and feet are black. The sexes are alike. Resident. Size 23 cms.

Rosy-patched Shrike
(Rhodophoneus cruent

A locally common bird in regions of dry thornbush and scrub, often encountered o
top of a bush from where they issue a loud, piping call. The male has the forehead,
crown, nape, mantle and wing and ear coverts greyish-brown. A broad band of
crimson red extends from the chin down the centre of the throat and breast, this
band is bordered by white feathering which also covers the belly and underparts.
The sides of the breast and the flanks have a wash of tawny-buff. The primary and
secondary wing feathers are dark grey-brown, the rump is crimson red and the tail i
black with white tips on the outermost feathers. The eyes are dark brown, the bill is
black and the legs and feet are grey. The female differs from the male in lacking the
crimson band on the white chin and upper throat, but has a broad black band across
the lower throat and a crimson band extending from it down the centre of the belly.
Resident. Size 23 cms.

Tropical Boubou
(Laniarius ferruginer

A widely distributed species in areas of forests, woodlands, scrub and thickets.
Rather shy birds that are usually in pairs skulking in dense vegetation, often being
located as a result of hearing the bell-like calls produced as a duet by a male and
female. The head, mantle, wings and tail are black with a sheen of blue, in some
individuals white is visible on the wing coverts. The chin, throat, breast, belly and
underparts are white, often with a wash of peach-buff on the breast and flanks. The
eyes are dark brown, the bill, legs and feet are black. The sexes are alike. Resident.
Size 23 cms.

Grey-headed Bush Shrike
(Malaconotus blanchot

A large, robust shrike with startling plumage, found in woodlands, riverine forests
and areas of scrub and bush. The head is a slaty blue-grey, the chin and throat are
bright yellow merging to chestnut on the breast then back to bright yellow on the
belly and underparts. The mantle, back, wings and tail are a bright rich green with
some yellow spotting on the wing coverts, secondary wing feathers and tail. The
eyes are yellow, the large, hooked bill is black and the legs and feet are grey-blue.
The sexes are alike. Resident. Size 25 cms.

Magpie Shrike

(Corvinella melano...

A very conspicuous shrike with a very long tail, usually encountered in pairs or small parties hunting insects from a vantage point on top of small bushes and ra... vegetation. Locally common over much of the region, favouring areas of open grassland with scattered scrub and woodland edges. The plumage is almost enti... glossy black, the exceptions being a broad white edge to the scapulars showing a... distinctive wing bar, white bases to the primary wing feathers, a white patch on t... flanks, a variable amount of white on the tip of the tail and a grey rump. The eyes... dark brown, the bill, legs and feet are black. The sexes are alike. Resident.
Size 38 cms.

European Red-backed Shrike

(Lanius coll...

Found over much of the region in a variety of habitats but preferring thornbush country and woodland edges. The male has a black band extending from the forehead, through the eye to the ear coverts, as if wearing a 'highwayman's mask'. The remainder of the head, nape and the rump are grey-blue. The chin and throat white, the breast, belly and underparts are white with a hint of pink. The mantle, wing coverts and secondary wing feathers are rich chestnut, the primary wing feathers are dark brown edged with chestnut. The tail feathers are black, the outermost feathers being white edged. The eyes are dark brown, the bill, legs and ... are black. The female lacks the splendour of the male, having a brown head, mant... and wing coverts, the underparts are off-white with crescents of brown on the sid... of the throat, breast, belly and flanks. Winter visitor. Size 17 cms.

Fiscal Shrike

(Lanius colla...

A widespread and common species over much of the region, often encountered around human habitations, cultivated farmland and woodland edges. The head, mantle and back are glossy black, the chin, cheeks, throat, breast, belly and underparts are white. The scapulars are black broadly edged with white resulting... a conspicuous wing bar. The rump is grey, the central tail feathers are black tipped with white and the outermost are black with broad white outer edges. The... eyes are dark brown, the bill, legs and feet are black. The female is similar to the male, but is occasionally brownish-black above and with some chestnut on the flanks. Resident. Size 23 cms.

Long-tailed Fiscal Shrike

(Lanius caban...

A widespread and locally common species, inhabiting grasslands and areas of scru... and bush. The forehead, crown and nape are black, the chin, cheeks, throat, breast and underparts are white. The mantle and scapulars are greyish, the wings are blac... with a small white patch at the base of the primary flight feathers. The rump is whi... the very long tail is black tipped with white. The eyes are dark brown, the bill, legs and feet are black. The sexes are alike. Resident. Size 30 cms.

Grey-backed Fiscal Shrike

(Lanius excubitoroid...

A bird of thornbush and acacia scrub, found in Uganda, western Tanzania and western Kenya from the rift valley lakes. A broad black band extends from the forehead, through the eye, ear coverts and down the sides of the neck. The crown, nape and mantle are silver-grey. The chin, cheeks, throat and underparts are white, as is the rump. The wings are black with a distinctive white patch at the base of the primary flight feathers. The long, broad tail is black tipped with white and the outermost feathers are white towards the base. The eyes are dark brown, the bill, leg... and feet are black. The sexes are similar. Resident. Size 25 cms.

Taita Fiscal Shrike

(Lanius dorsali...

A reasonably common bird in areas of dry bush country, often perching conspicuously on the upper most branches of bushes from where they drop on prey items. The forehead, upper face, crown and nape are black, the chin, cheeks, breast, belly and underparts are white. The mantle is grey merging with the white of the back and rump. The wings are totally black, the broad tail is black narrowly tipped and edged with white. The eyes are dark brown, the bill, legs and feet are black. The sexes are alike. Resident. Size 20 cms.

Stonechat
(Saxicola torq

A reasonably common species at elevations of 1500 metres or more, inhabiting ar
of open country with low scrub, moorlands and woodland forest edges. The male
the head, nape, mantle, chin and throat black, the centre of the breast is rich ches
The sides of the neck and breast are white, as are the belly and underparts. The w
coverts are black edged with white forming a distinctive wing bar when perched.
primary and secondary wing feathers are black, the uppertail coverts and rump s
white, the tail is black. The eyes are dark brown, the bill, legs and feet are black. T
female has the upper plumage warm brown-black. Resident. Size 13 cms.

Schalow's Wheatear
(Oenanthe lu

Quite common in highland areas, on rocky hill sides, cliffs or bare stony ground.
forehead, crown and nape are creamy-white, the chin, throat, face, neck, mantle
wings are black. The breast, belly and underparts are white, often with a wash of
buff. The rump is whitish, the tail is black with white on the basal half of the oute
feathers. The eyes are dark brown, the bill, legs and feet are black. The female has
upper plumage grey-brown and the chin and throat greyish. Resident. Size 15 cm

Common Wheatear
(Oenanthe oenar

A common winter visitor to much of the region on short grass plains and savanna
dry rocky areas and cultivated farmland. The male has the forehead, crown, nape
and mantle greyish. A black band extends from the base of the bill through the ey
before broadening to cover the ear coverts. (In breeding plumage this area of black
also covers the chin and throat). The chin is white, the throat and breast are white
washed with warm buff. The belly and underparts are greyish-white. The primary
and secondary wing feathers are black edged with buff. The rump is white and th
tail is black, tipped with white and with the basal portion of the outer feathers wh
The eyes are dark brown, the bill. legs and feet are black. The female has the
upperparts buff-brown and has the black facial patch of the male replaced with pa
olive-brown. Palearctic winter visitor. Size 15 cms.

Isabeline Wheatear
(Oenanthe isabell

A winter visitor to areas of semi-desert and open plains in Kenya, Uganda and
northern Tanzania. A bird with almost uniform sandy-brown plumage both above
and below. A faint eye stripe is present and the belly and underparts have a cream
wash. The primary and secondary wing feathers are dark brown edged with buff.
The rump is white and the tail feathers are white at the bases and black at the tips.
The eyes are dark brown, the bill,legs and feet are black. The sexes are alike.
Palearctic winter visitor. Size 16 cms.

Pied Wheatear
(Oenanthe pleschan

A common winter visitor to much of the region. The forehead, crown and nape are
brownish on arrival in the autumn, becoming whiter throughout the winter in
readiness for their spring migration north. The face, cheeks, chin and throat are
black-brown. The breast, belly and underparts are buff-white, the lower breast
sometimes showing traces of creamy-yellow. The wings are black-brown, and the
rump is white. The basal half of the central tail feathers are white with the remaini
half black, while the outer feathers are almost completely white with black tips. Th
eyes are dark brown, the bill, legs and feet are black. The female has upperparts
mottled brown and the throat and breast greyish-brown. Palearctic winter visitor.
Size 14 cms.

Capped Wheatear
(Oenanthe pileat

A common species on short grass plains and savannahs in central and southern
Kenya and throughout Tanzania. The forehead is white with a band following the
line of the eyebrow. The crown is black, merging with the chocolate brown of the
nape, mantle, back and wing coverts. The cheeks and sides of the neck are black,
joining with a black breast bib. The chin, throat, belly and underparts are white wit
a wash of cream-buff on the flanks. The wing feathers are dark brown-black edged
with buff. The rump is white, the tail is predominantly black with white at the base.
The eyes are dark brown, the bill is black and the legs and feet are greyish-black. Th
sexes are alike. Resident. Size 16 cms.

Anteater Chat
(Myrmecocichla aet.)

A very common species in south-western and central Kenya, particularly in the Masai Mara and in the highlands of northern Tanzania. They are often encounte along the margins of roads and tracks. A sturdy bird with the entire plumage brownish-black, the only exception being the primary wing feathers which are v at the base, showing as a very conspicuous wing bar in flight. The flight itself is rather weak and laboured. The eyes are dark brown, the bill, legs and feet are bla The sexes are alike. It is possible to confuse this species with the Sooty Chat (*Myrmecocichla nigra*) which has white wing coverts not primaries, the female a immature Sooty Chat have no white in the wings at all. Resident. Size 20 cms.

Sooty Chat
(Myrmecocichla n)

A bird of open plains and grasslands with scattered bush and scrub, in south-western Kenya, north-western and southern Tanzania and throughout most of Uganda. The plumage of the male is entirely black with the exception of the wing coverts which are white. The female and immature birds are dark brown and hav white in the wings at all. The eyes are dark brown, the bill, legs and feet are black This species may be confused with the Anteater Chat (*Myrmecocichla aethiops*) which has the base of the primary wing feathers white. Resident. Size 18 cms.

Cliffchat
(Myrmecocichla cinnamomeiver)

As it's name implies this species can be found on cliffs, escarpment edges and rock hill sides. The male has the head, mantle, chin, throat and breast glossy black. A narrow white band separates the black breast from the rich orange-red of the belly underparts. The wing coverts are white, the remainder of the wings are black. The rump is orange-red and the tail is black. The female has the head, mantle, chin, thre and breast dark slaty-grey and, unlike the male, shows no white on the wing covert The eyes are dark brown, the bill, legs and feet are black. Resident.Size 20 cms.

European Redstart
(Phoenicurus phoenicu)

A winter visitor to many parts of East Africa. The male has the forehead white and the crown, mantle and wing coverts slaty-grey. The face, chin and throat are black the breast is orange-red becoming paler on the belly and underparts. The primary and secondary wing feathers are dark brown edged and tipped with buff-white. Th rump and outer tail feathers are orange-red, the central tail feathers are black. The female (illustrated) has grey-brown upper plumage, sandy brown below with whit on the belly. The rump and tail are orange-red with the central tail feathers black a in the male. The eyes are dark brown, the bill, legs and feet are black. Palearctic winter visitor. Size 14 cms.

Red-backed Scrub Robin
(Cercotrichas leucophr)

A species found over much of the region in areas of bush, open woodland and dens thickets and scrub. The forehead, crown and nape are grey-brown. A white stripe follows the line of the eyebrow from the base of the bill, the chin and throat are whi with a black moustachial stripe. The breast is white, boldly streaked with dark grey the belly and underparts are white with a wash of warm buff on the flanks. The win coverts and secondary wing feathers are dark brown-black broadly tipped with white. The primary wing feathers are black edged with russet brown. The rump an tail are russet brown, the latter tipped black and white. The eyes are dark brown, th bill, legs and feet are black. The sexes are alike. Resident. Size 15 cms.

Spotted Morning Warbler
(Cichladusa guttat)

A shy, secretive inhabitant of dry bush, scrub, thickets and dense undergrowth in savannahs, parks and gardens. The forehead and crown are brown streaked with grey-white, the nape, mantle, back, rump and tail are russet brown. A narrow white stripe follows the line of the eyebrow and the cheeks, chin and throat are buff-white with a black moustachial stripe. The breast, belly and underparts are buff-white, the breast, belly and flanks being boldly spotted with black. The wings are brown with the primary and secondary feathers edged russet brown. The eyes are dark brown, the bill, legs and feet are black. The sexes are alike. Resident. Size 17 cms.

Heuglin's Robin Chat
(Cossypha heug

Distributed over much of the region, favouring woodlands and gardens with dens
undercover. A rather shy, secretive species, often seen skulking about under bush
and shrubs. The forehead, crown and nape are black and a broad white band follo
the line of the eyebrow to the side of the nape. The face, upper cheeks and ear cove
are black. The chin, lower cheeks, throat, neck, breast and underparts are rich oran
red. The mantle, back and scapulars are olive-brown, the wing coverts and primar
and secondary wing feathers are slaty-brown. The rump is orange-red. The central
feathers are olive brown and the outer feathers are dull orange-red. The eyes are da
brown, the bill is black and the legs and feet are mid-brown. The female is
occasionally browner on the mantle and back, otherwise the sexes are alike. It is ea
to confuse this species with Ruppell's Robin Chat (*Cossypha semirufa*) which has t
wings dark olive brown and the central tail feathers black. Resident. Size 20 cms.

Ruppell's Robin Chat
(Cossypha semir

A bird of forests, thickets and the dense undergrowth of woodlands and gardens ir
the highlands of central and southern Kenya and north-central Tanzania. The
forehead, crown and nape are black, a white stripe extends from the sides of the
forehead above the eye to the hind-neck. The face, cheeks, sides of the neck and ea
coverts are black. The chin, throat, breast, belly and underparts are orange-red. Th
mantle, back and scapulars are olive brown, the wing coverts an primary and
secondary wing feathers are dark brown edged with olive. The rump and outer tail
feathers are orange-red, the central tail feathers are black. The eyes are dark brown
the bill is black and the legs and feet are mid-brown. The sexes are alike. This spec
could easily be mistaken for the Heuglin's Robin Chat (*Cossypha heuglini*) which i
larger and has slaty-brown wings and olive brown central tail feathers. Resident.
Size 18 cms.

Olive Thrush
(Turdus olivacer

A bird of forests, woodlands, hill sides and gardens with trees, bushes and dense
undergrowth. Somewhat shy and secretive they spend much of their time skulking
in deep vegetation. The head, back, mantle and wing coverts are olive brown, paler
on the cheeks and sides of the neck. The chin and throat are white streaked with da
brown, the breast is grey brown often with dark brown and whitish streaks. The sid
of the belly and the flanks are orange-red, the centre of the belly and underparts
showing some white. The wing coverts are greyish-brown and the primary and
secondary wing feathers are dark brown edged with olive. The tail is greyish-brown
The eyes are dark brown, with a bright yellow-orange orbital ring. The bill, legs and
feet are orange-yellow. The sexes are alike. Immature birds have the chin, throat,
breast and flanks spotted with black. Resident. Size 23 cms.

Bare-eyed Thrush
(Turdus tephronotu

One of East Africa's most attractive thrushes, found in areas of dry bush and scrub
particularly along the coasts of Kenya, northern Tanzania and southern Somalia,
also inland as far as the central highlands. The head, nape, mantle, wing coverts and
upper breast are slaty blue-grey. The chin and throat are white boldly streaked with
black. The lower breast, belly and underparts are orange-red. The primary and
secondary wing feathers are blackish edged with grey-blue. The tail is slaty blue-
grey. The eyes are dark brown surrounded by an area of bare yellow-orange skin. The
bill is bright orange and the legs and feet are yellow-orange. The sexes are alike.
Immature birds have the breast streaked and spotted black. Resident. Size 21 cms.

Arrow-marked Babbler
(Turdoides jard...)

A bird of bush, scrub, light woodlands, swamp edges and dense undergrowth throughout much of the region. Usually encountered in small but noisy parties, foraging from bush to bush. The feathers of the head and neck are dark brown edged with buff-white, the lores are dark. The chin, throat, breast and belly are greyish-brown, the chin, throat and breast having the feathers tipped with white. The central tail and primary wing feathers are dark brown, the remainder of the tail and wings are ashy-brown. The eyes are bright yellow-orange, the bill is black and the legs and feet are grey. The sexes are alike. Resident. Size 23 cms.

Black-lored Babbler
(Turdoides melan...)

Locally common in woodlands, bush, scrub and areas of dense vegetation around swamp and lake edges. Often encountered in small, noisy parties. The head, neck, chin and throat feathers are dark grey broadly edged, tipped and streaked with grey white. The lores are black, contrasting quite strongly with the remainder of the head. The feathers of the breast, belly and underparts are ashy-brown edged with grey. The wings and tail are ashy-brown. The eyes are cream-white, the bill, legs and feet are black. The sexes are alike. Resident. Size 23 cms.

Rufous Chatterer
(Turdoides rubigino...)

A species found in dry thickets, bush and scrub over much of the region, often foraging through the undergrowth in small parties. The forehead, crown, nape and ear coverts are grey-brown, the forehead often being streaked with white. The feathers of the chin, throat and centre of the breast are pale rust-red with narrow white streaks. The outer breast, belly and underparts are rusty-red. The mantle, wings and long tail are ashy-brown. The eyes are cream-white, the bill, legs and feet are flesh-grey. The sexes are alike. Resident. Size 19 cms.

European Sedge Warbler
(Acrocephalus schoenobaenu...)

A common winter visitor to East Africa, frequenting swamps, reed beds and other waterside vegetation. The forehead, crown and nape are brown streaked with black, a broad whitish band extends from the base of the bill, over the eye to the side of the nape. The chin, throat and central upper breast are off-white, the remainder of the breast, the belly and underparts are off-white with a wash of buff, darkest on the flanks. The mantle, scapulars and wings are ashy-brown with dark brown streaks and edges. The rump is rufous brown and the rounded tail is dark brown. The bill is black and the legs and feet are flesh-grey. The sexes are alike. Palearctic winter visitor. Size 13 cms.

Reed Warbler
(Acrocephalus scirpaceus)

A winter visitor to the region, where they inhabit areas of swamp and lake edges. Usually quite secretive, skulking in reedbeds and other thick waterside vegetation. They also occupy areas of acacia bush and scrub. The upper plumage is a uniform olive-brown/grey, often with a rusty coloured rump, the primary and secondary flight feathers are a darker brown/grey. A lighter eyebrow stripe and eye ring are discernable at close quarters. The eyes are dark brown, the bill is dark brown/grey and pale yellow at the base, the legs and feet are flesh/grey. The sexes are alike. Palearctic winter visitor. Size 13 cms.

Willow Warbler
(Phylloscopus trochilus)

A winter visitor throughout much of the region, found in a wide variety of habitats. The forehead, crown, nape, mantle, wings and tail are plain olive-brown, lighter on the rump. A pale whitish stripe follows the line of the eyebrow from the base of the bill. The chin, throat, breast, belly and underparts are whitish with a wash of pale yellow-buff on the sides of the breast, belly and flanks. The eyes are dark brown, the bill is brown-yellow and the legs and feet are grey-brown. The sexes are alike. Palearctic winter visitor. Size 11 cms.

Winding Cisticola
(Cisticola galact

A locally common species throughout the region, favouring swamps, marshes an
areas of dense rank grasses, usually in the vicinity of water. The forehead, crown a
nape are russet brown, the ear coverts are buff/brown. The chin, throat and breast
white, the underparts are white with a wash of buff. The mantle and back are grey
streaked with black. The wing coverts and the primary and secondary flight feath
are dark brown/black edged with russet brown and buff. The rump is plain grey, t
tail feathers are brown/black edged with russet brown and with bold white spots
towards the tip. The eyes are brown, the bill dull grey and the legs and feet pale fl
pink. The sexes are alike. Resident. Size 13 cms.

Pectoral-patch Cisticola
(Cisticola brunnesc

Found throughout much of the region in areas of open grassland and savannah. Th
forehead and crown are plain buff, edged with streaks of brown. The nape and ear
coverts are buff, finely streaked with brown. The chin, throat, breast, belly and
underparts are white washed with buff. A pectoral patch of dark brown/black is
present on either side of the neck and chest. The mantle, back and wings are buff,
heavily streaked with brown/black. The tail is brown streaked with black and edge
with buff. The eyes are dark brown, the bill is grey/brown and the legs and feet are
pale flesh pink. The female is similar to the male but the pectoral patches are less
prominent or even absent. Resident. Size 9 cms.

Black-collared Apalis
(Apalis pulch

A bird of highland forests and woodlands throughout Uganda and western and
central Kenya. They usually carry their tails 'cocked' upwards towards the back,
fanning and waving them from side to side. The forehead, crown, nape and back ar
dark slaty-grey. The chin and throat are white and a broad black band extends acros
the upper breast. The lower breast is white and the flanks, belly and underparts are
rich chestnut brown. The wings are dark slaty-grey. The rump and tail are grey, the
latter tipped white. The eyes are dark brown, the bill legs and feet are grey/black.
The sexes are alike. Resident. Size 13 cms.

Grey-capped Warbler
(Hypergerus lepid

A rather shy stocky warbler, widely distributed and usually encountered in dense,
luxuriant undergrowth along the edges of lakes, rivers and streams. The forehead
and crown are blue/grey, bordered by a broad black band extending from the lores,
through the eye to the nape. The chin, breast, belly and underparts are pale grey and
the centre of the throat has a prominent patch of chestnut. The mantle, back, wings,
rump and tail are rich olive-green, a patch of chestnut is sometimes visible on the
shoulder of the wing. The eyes are dark brown, the bill is black and the legs and feet
are dull red. The sexes are alike. Resident. Size 15 cms.

Grey-backed Camaroptera
(Camaroptera brachyura

A shy, secretive little bird that spends much of it's time skulking in dense bush and
scrub. They usually carry the tail 'cocked' upwards towards the back. Widely
distributed over much of the region. The head, mantle, rump, tail and underparts are
grey. The chin, throat and breast are pale grey. The wing coverts and flight feathers
are rich olive-green. The eyes are red, the bill is black and the legs and feet are dull
brown/red. The sexes are alike. Resident. Size 10 cms.

Red-faced Crombec
(Sylvietta whytii,

Distributed over much of the region in areas of acacia thornbush and scrub. A small
warbler with a very short tail. The crown, nape, mantle, wings and tail are pale grey.
The forehead, cheeks, neck, breast, belly, flanks and underparts are rufous brown.
The eyes are dark brown, the bill is grey/black and the legs and feet are deep red. The
sexes are alike. This species can be confused with the Crombec (*Sylvietta brachyura*)
which is smaller and has the chin, throat, eyebrow stripe, belly and underparts
white. Resident. Size 10 cms.

Dusky Flycatcher
(Muscicapa adu

A widely distributed species favouring areas of open forests and woodlands, also often encountered in large parks and gardens. They can often be seen hawking for insects from a favoured perch. The head, nape, mantle, back and wing coverts are plain greyish-brown. The chin, throat, breast, belly and underparts are white, the flanks and sides of the breast having a wash of grey/buff. The flight and tail feathe are dark grey/brown. The eyes are dark brown, the bill, legs and feet are dark grey/black. The sexes are alike. Immature birds have the upperparts spotted with buff and some dark streaking below. Resident. Size 10 cms.

European Spotted Flycatcher
(Muscicapa stri

A common winter visitor over much of the region in areas of thornbush and scrub. The forehead and crown are pale grey/brown streaked with dark brown. The ear coverts and cheeks are pale brown. The chin, throat and breast are white, streaked with brown, the belly and underparts are white. The mantle, back, scapulars and rump are grey/brown. The primary and secondary flight feathers are dark brown, narrowly edged with buff and white. The tail feathers are dark brown. The eyes are dark brown, the bill, legs and feet are black. The sexes are alike. Palearctic winter visitor. Size 13 cms.

White-eyed Slaty Flycatcher
(Melaenornis fische

Found over much of the region in highland forests and woodlands as well as in parks, gardens and areas of cultivated land. Typical of flycatchers they can often be seen hawking for insects from a favoured perch. The head, mantle, back and wings are slaty-grey. The chin and throat are pale grey, the breast, belly and underparts ar white with a wash of grey/buff along the flanks. The most prominent identification feature is the broad white eye-ring. The eyes are dark brown, the bill, legs and feet are dark grey/black. The sexes are alike. Immature birds have the upperparts spotte with white. Resident. Size 15 cms.

Grey Flycatcher
(Bradornis microrhynchi

Found in areas of dry thornbush and savannah woodlands throughout Ethiopia, Uganda, Kenya and Tanzania. A rather drab flycatcher with the plumage of the upperparts a rather uniform dull grey. The forehead and crown have some indistinc dark streaking. The chin, throat, breast, belly and underparts are whitish-grey. The eyes are dark brown, the bill, legs and feet are dark grey/black. The sexes are alike. Immature birds have white/buff spotting and streaking over the upper plumage and some dark streaking on the breast. Resident. Size 13 cms.

Wattle-eye Flycatcher
(Platysteira cyane

A bird of forests and woodlands in western Kenya, Uganda and northern Tanzania. very striking flycatcher with the male having the forehead, crown, nape, mantle and back blue/black. The chin, throat, lower breast, belly and underparts are white, with a broad blue/black band extending across the upper breast. The female has a greyish blue/black head and mantle, while the throat and upper breast are a rich chestnut brown. Both sexes have a prominent red eye-wattle. A white wing bar is present across the secondary flight feathers, the primary wing and tail feathers are black edged with white. The eyes are dark brown, the bill, legs and feet are black. Residen Size 13 cms.

Paradise Flycatcher
(Tersiphone viridi

A widespread and common species throughout the region in woodlands, thickets and areas of scrub. The head and neck are blue/black, merging to slaty-grey on the chin, throat and breast, becoming white on the belly and underparts. The eyes have a blue orbital ring. The mantle, back, wing coverts and tail are rich chestnut red. The central tail feathers of the male become elongated during the breeding season making identification even easier. The secondary flight feathers are chestnut edged with white, the primary flight feathers are black. In some regions, principally easter Kenya, a white phase occurs. This affects the males only, to the extent that all areas of chestnut plumage found in the nominant phase are white. The eyes are dark brown, the bill, legs and feet are grey/black. Resident. Size: Male including tail 33 cms, female 20 cms.

Scarlet-chested Sunbird
(Nectarinia senegale

Encountered in a wide variety of habitats. The male has the upper plumage dark brown/black. The crown, chin and throat are bright metallic green and the breast vivid scarlet. The belly and underparts are dark brown/black. The female lacks the bright plumage of the male, being dusky-olive above with a flush of dark brown on the wings and tail. The underparts are pale yellow/buff streaked with brown. The eyes are dark brown, the long, decurved bill and the legs and feet are black. Reside Size 15 cms.

Hunter's Sunbird
(Nectarinia hunt

A bird of dry thornbush country. The male has the upper plumage glossy black, which often shows a sheen of metallic violet/purple. The forehead, crown and moustachial stripe are bright metallic green, the chin, throat, belly and underparts are black. The breast is a vivid scarlet. The female lacks the bright iridescent plumage of the male, being ashy-brown above and pale yellow/buff below with so brown streaking on the breast, throat and chin. The eyes are dark brown, the decurved bill, the legs and the feet are black. Resident. Size 14 cms.

Variable Sunbird
(Nectarinia venus

A common species over much of the region. The male has the upper plumage bright metallic blue/green, the primary and secondary flight feathers are brown. The chin, throat and upper breast are dark purple/blue, the lower breast, belly and underparts a yellow. There is, however, much regional variation in the plumage of the underparts, ranging from white, through yellow to pale orange. The female (illustrated) has the upper plumage ashy-grey, often showing a pale eyebrow stripe, and is yellow/white below. The eyes are dark brown, the decurved bill and the legs and feet are black. resident. Size 9 cms.

Bronze Sunbird
(Nectarinia kilimens

A common bird of Uganda and the highland regions of Kenya and Tanzania. The male has the head and neck dull metallic green, the remainder of the upper plumag being dull metallic bronze. The wings and elongated tail are dull purple/black. The chin and throat are bronze, merging to purple/black on the breast, belly and underparts. The female has the upper plumage olive/ashy-grey, while the underpar are yellowish streaked with bronze-grey. The female (illustrated) lacks the elongate tail feathers of the male. The eyes are dark brown, the decurved bill is black and the legs and feet are greyish-black. Resident. Size: Male 23 cms, female 14 cms.

Beautiful Sunbird
(Nectarinia pulchell

A locally common species throughout much of the region away from coastal districts. The male, in breeding plumage, has the head, neck, mantle, back and wing coverts bright metallic green. the chin, throat and upper breast are metallic green, the centre of the lower breast is bright scarlet being bordered on either side by patches of bright yellow. The belly and underparts are metallic green/black. The primary and secondary flight feathers are blue/black. The tail is blue/black with the elongated central feathers edged with metallic green. In non breeding plumage male appear similar to females but retain the long central tail feathers and the dark flight feathers. The female has the upper plumage ashy-grey. The chin and throat are white, becoming pale yellow on the breast, belly and underparts. The female lacks the elongated tail feathers of the male. The eyes are dark brown, the decurved bill, the legs and the feet are black. Resident. Size: Male 15 cms, female 11 cms.

Kenya Violet-backed Sunbird
(Anthreptes orientalis

A locally common species inhabiting areas of semi-desert thornbush country, much attracted to flowering acacia trees. The male has the head, mantle, back, tail and wing coverts metallic violet/blue. The flight feathers are dark brown/black. The rump and shoulders of the wings are metallic green. The chin and upper throat are blue/black, the lower throat, breast, belly and underparts are white. A small patch of yellow is present on the sides of the breast. The female is ashy-grey above with a pale eyebrow stripe, the tail is purple/black and the wings are brownish-grey. The chin, throat, breast, belly and underparts are white, occasionally with a faint wash of yellow. The eyes are dark brown, the bill is brown/black, the legs and feet are black. Resident. Size 11 cms.

Kikuyu White-eye
(Zosterops poliogaster kikuyue

A species often encountered in flocks, in highland forests and woodlands, particularly in the Aberdare Mountains of southern/central Kenya, the Ngorongo highlands of northern Tanzania and the highlands of north western Uganda. The forehead is bright yellow, the crown, nape, mantle and upperparts are olive green Around the eye is a broad, conspicuous white ring. The chin, throat and breast are yellow, the belly, flanks and underparts are olive green. The eyes are dark brown, bill, legs and feet are greyish-black. the sexes are alike. Resident. Size 11 cms.

Golden-breasted Bunting
(Emberiza flavivent

A widely, but locally distributed species, inhabiting dry areas of forest, woodland and scrub. The head is black, with white stripes extending above and below the ey and down the centre of the head from the forehead to the nape. The chin is white, throat and breast are orange/yellow, the belly and underparts are white with a was of grey. The mantle and back are rufous brown, the rump is grey, the wing coverts a rufous tipped with white and the primary and secondary wing feathers are brown/black edged with white. The tail is black, the outer feathers being edged wi white. The eyes are dark brown. The bill has the upper mandible black and the low mandible pale pink. the legs and feet are flesh-pink. The sexes are similar, the fem being slightly duller and, having those areas of black plumage found in the male, replaced with brown. Resident. Size 15 cms.

Yellow-fronted Canary
(Serinus mozambic

Locally distributed throughout the region, favouring woodlands, areas of scrub, cultivated farmland and parks and gardens. The forehead and eyebrow stripe are bright yellow, the crown, nape, mantle, back and wing coverts are olive green streaked with black. They have a black moustachial stripe and a dark stripe extending from the base of the bill through the eye.. The rump is bright yellow, the tail feathers are dark, the outer feathers being edged with olive green/yellow. The primary and secondary wing feathers are blackish, edged with yellow/green. The eyes are dark brown, the bill pale brown and the legs and feet brown/black. The sexes are similar, the female usually having a browner head and mantle. Resident. Size 11 cms.

African Citril
(Serinus citrinelloide

A species distributed over much of the region, inhabiting forest and woodland edge and clearings, cultivated farmland, grasslands with some bush and scrub cover and gardens. The forehead, face, cheeks, chin and upper throat are black. They have a yellow eyebrow stripe. The lower throat, breast, belly and underparts are lemon yellow, with a variable amount of dark streaking usually heaviest on the flanks. The crown, nape, mantle and wing coverts are olive green streaked with black. The tail and the primary and secondary flight feathers are blackish edged with greenish-yellow. The eyes are dark brown, the bill is blood red/black, the legs and feet are black. The female lacks the black facial feathering of the male. Resident. Size 11 cm

Streaky Seed-eater
(Serinus striolatu

A common, well distributed species throughout the region, inhabiting woodland and forest edges, areas of scrub and bush, cultivated farmland and parks and gardens. The forehead, crown, nape, mantle and wing coverts are mid-brown streaked with black. A white stripe follows the line of the eyebrow from the base of the bill to the ear coverts. The chin and throat are buff/white, the moustachial stripe is brown/black. The breast, belly and underparts are white/buff, heavily streaked with black. The tail and the primary and secondary wing feathers are dark brown edged with buff and white. The eyes are dark brown, the bill is pink/yellow and the legs and feet are blackish. The sexes are alike. Resident. Size 15 cms.

Common Waxbill
(Estrilda ast

A common species throughout the region, usually encountered in areas of rank grassland. The male has the forehead, crown and nape dark brown closely barred with grey/brown. A broad red stripe extends from the base of the bill, through the eye to the ear coverts. The cheeks, chin and throat are white. The centre of the breast and belly are pale red, the sides of the breast and the flanks are buff/white closely barred with dark brown. The remainder of the underparts are black. The mantle, back, wings and tail are dark brown, barred with grey/buff. The female has less red and black on the breast, belly and underparts. The eyes are dark brown, the bill is red (black in the immature) and the legs and feet are black. Resident. Size 10 cms.

Purple Grenadier
(Uraeginthus ianthinogast

A species found in areas of dry thornbush, thick scrub and open bush habitats over much of the region. A bird of striking plumage, the male has a narrow iridescent bl band across the forehead which extends onto the sides of the head to encircle the eyes and cover the cheeks. The crown, nape, neck, chin, throat and upper breast are rich russet brown. The lower breast, belly and underparts are violet blue, the mantle back and wings are brown, the rump is violet blue and the tail is black. The female has the area around the eyes pale blue/white and the breast, belly and underparts dull russet brown with white spots and barring. The eyes are dark red, the bill is bright pinkish-red and the legs and feet are black. Resident. Size 14 cms.

Red-cheeked Cordon-bleu
(Uraeginthus bengalu

Distributed over much of the region, favouring grasslands with some bush cover. Usually encountered feeding on or near the ground in small flocks. The forehead, crown, nape, mantle and wings are sandy-brown. The face, chin, throat, sides of the breast, belly and underparts are azure blue. A bright scarlet patch covers the ear coverts. The centre of the breast, belly and underparts are buff/brown. The rump and tail are bright blue. The female is generally duller in appearance than the male and lacks the scarlet patch on the ear coverts. The bill is pink with a black tip, the legs and feet are flesh-pink. Resident. Size 13 cms.

Red-billed Firefinch
(Lagonosticta senegala

Widely distributed within the region. A very small finch, often seen in flocks feeding on the ground. The male has the entire head, neck, mantle, chin, throat and breast red. Generally a few white spots are discernable on the sides of the breast. The belly and underparts are sandy-brown. The wing coverts are red, the primary and secondary wing feathers are dull brown. The rump and outer tail feathers are red, the central tail feathers are brown. The female lacks the red plumage of the male except on the lores, the rump and the tail, being earth-brown above and buff below with white spots on the sides of the breast and flanks. The eyes are dark red, the bill is red and the legs and feet are greyish-pink. Resident. Size 9 cms.

Silverbill
(Lonchura cantans)

A common species often encountered feeding together in small flocks in dry bush country throughout Uganda, Kenya and northern Tanzania. The head, chin and throat are dark brown finely streaked with ashy-brown. They have a pale blue orbital ring. The breast, belly and underparts are white. The wing coverts and secondary flight feathers are dark brown with ashy-grey vermiculations. The primary flight feathers, the rump and the pointed tail are black. The eyes are dark brown, the thick bill is blue/grey and the legs and feet are flesh pink/grey. The sexes are alike. Resident. Size 10 cms.

Bronze Mannikin
(Lonchura cucullata)

A common bird over much of the region, found in a wide variety of habitats including dry thornbush country, cultivated farmland, grasslands, river banks, lake and stream edges and in parks and gardens. The forehead, crown, cheeks, chin and throat are glossy black, merging to bronze on the ear coverts, neck and nape. The breast, belly and underparts are white with black barring on the flanks and under tail coverts. The mantle, back and wing coverts are ashy-brown, the flight feathers are dark brown. The rump is white boldly barred with black, the tail is black. The eyes are dark brown, the bill is blue/black and the legs and feet are blackish. The sexes are alike. Resident. Size 9 cms.

Pin-tailed Whydah
(Vidua macro

A parasitic species laying it's eggs in the nests of Waxbills, Finches and Cisticolas. The breeding male is almost unmistakable, the forehead, crown and chin are black the nape, neck, breast, belly and underparts are white. The mantle, shoulders and back are black, the wing coverts are white and the primary and secondary wing feathers are black edged with buff/white. The outer tail feathers are black edged with white, the black central tail feathers are elongated, measuring almost twice the length of the body.In non-breeding dress the males look similar to females, having the forehead and crown tawny-brown with bold black stripes extending from the to the nape. The throat, breast, belly and underparts are white with a wash of buff, the mantle, back and wings are tawny-brown broadly streaked with black. The tail brown/black edged with white and lacks the elongated central feathers. The eyes dark brown, the bill is pink/red and the legs and feet are flesh pink. Resident. Size breeding male 32 cms, female 12 cms.

Paradise Whydah
(Vidua paradisa

Locally distributed over much of the region in areas of savannah bush, acacia thorn and scrub. A parasitic species, laying it's eggs in the nests of Green-winged Pytilia. The breeding male has the entire head, chin, throat and upper breast black, the nape is buff and forms a collar around the neck to the breast. The lower breast is chestnut merging to buff/white on the belly and underparts. The mantle, back, wings and tai are black. The central tail feathers are relatively short but extremely broad, the outer feathers are greatly elongated being over twice the length of the body. The non-breeding plumage of the males resembles that of the females, having the head creamy-buff with broad black stripes extending from the bill to the nape. The throat breast, belly and underparts are buff/white, with dark streaking on the flanks and the sides of the breast. The mantle, back and wing coverts are tawny streaked with black the flight feathers and tail are brown/black finely edged with buff. The eyes are dark brown, the bill is black and the legs and feet are brown/grey. Resident. Size; breeding male 40 cms, female 13 cms.

Reichnow's Weaver
(Ploceus baglafecht reichnow

Locally distributed at elevations of 1200 metres and above. The male has the forehead and fore-crown bright golden yellow, the hind-crown and nape are black. A broad black facial mask covers the lores, the eyes and the ear coverts. The chin, throat, breast, belly and underparts are bright yellow. The mantle, back and wing coverts are black. The primary and secondary wing feathers are black broadly edged with yellow. The tail is black. The female lacks the golden yellow forehead and crown, having the entire head black. The eyes are pale yellow, the bill is black and the legs and feet are flesh pink. Resident. Size 15 cms.

Golden Palm Weaver
(Ploceus bojeri)

A common species. The male has the head, neck, chin, throat and upper breast bright orange/yellow, the remainder of the plumage being bright yellow. The primary and secondary wing feathers and the tail are dark brown broadly edged with yellow. The female is yellow below, the upper plumage being yellow washed with olive and finely streaked with olive-brown. The eyes are dark brown, the bill is black in the male and yellow/grey in the female, the legs and feet are flesh pink. Resident. Size 15 cms.

Northern Masked Weaver
(Ploceus taeniopterus)

A weaver of lake edges and swamps with limited local distribution. The breeding male has the forehead black, becoming chestnut on the fore-crown. The hind-crown, nape, sides of the neck, breast, belly and underparts are bright yellow. A black face-mask covers the lores, eyes, cheeks, chin and upper throat. The mantle and wing coverts are yellow with a wash of olive, the primary and secondary wing feathers are dark brown, broadly edged with yellow. The rump is bright yellow and the tail is olive-brown edged with yellow. In non-breeding plumage the males are similar to the females, having the head olive/yellow finely streaked and flecked with black, the breast, belly and underparts are buff/white. The mantle and wing coverts are brown/black edged with buff. The eyes are deep red, the bill is black and the legs and feet are flesh pink. Resident. Size 15 cms.

Speke's Weaver
(Ploceus sp

An abundant species found in a variety of habitats including light woodlands, swamps, farmland and around human habitations. The male has the forehead, crown, nape and neck yellow. The chin, throat, face and cheeks are black, the bre belly and underparts are yellow, often with a wash of orange on the lower throat a upper breast. The feathers of the back and wing coverts are dark brown broadly edged with yellow, the primary and secondary flight feathers are dark brown fine edged with pale yellow. The rump is olive yellow and the tail feathers are dark brown edged with olive. The female is grey brown above streaked with dark brow the underparts are pale yellow/white. The eyes are yellow, the bill, legs and feet a blackish with a hint of pink/red. Resident. Size 15 cms.

Layard's Black-headed Weaver
(Ploceus cucullatus nigric

Encountered over much of the region in areas of bush and scrub, light woodlands and in the vicinity of human habitations. The male has the head, chin, throat and centre of the upper breast black. The hind neck, lower breast, belly and underpart are bright yellow. The wing coverts are dark brown/black broadly edged with yell the primary and secondary flight feathers are black narrowly edged with pale yellow/white. The tail is dark olive brown. The female is olive brown above with darker brown streaking and off-white below with a wash of pale yellow on the thro and upper breast. The eyes are red, the bill is black and the legs and feet are dull reddish/black. Resident. Size 16 cms.

Spectacled Weaver
(Ploceus ocular

Locally common throughout much of the region, inhabiting areas of forest, woodland and scrub usually in close proximity to water. The male has the head, neck, lower breast, belly and underparts bright yellow, often with a flush of orange on the forehead and crown. A narrow black eye stripe extends from the lores to the ear coverts. The chin, throat and central upper breast are black. The mantle, back, wings and tail are yellow/green, the primary and secondary flight feathers being narrowly edged with yellow. The female is similar to the male but lacks the black chin/throat bib. The eyes are pale yellow, the bill, legs and feet are black. Resident. Size 15 cms.

Golden-backed Weaver
(Ploceus jackson

A bird of scrub, bush and thickets in the immediate vicinity of lakes, rivers and swamps. The male has the entire head, including the chin and throat black, the breast and flanks are rich dark chestnut, the belly and underparts are yellow. The mantle and back are bright yellow, the wings and tail are olive brown narrowly edged with yellow. The female is olive yellow above with a variable amount of darker streaking, while below the breast is yellow becoming paler, almost white, on the belly and underparts. The eyes are crimson red, the bill, legs and feet are dull flesh-pink to black. Resident. Size 15 cms.

Red-headed Weaver
(Anaplectes rubiceps

Widely distributed over the region, favouring acacia woodland and scrub. The male has the head, neck, throat, breast and upper belly bright crimson red. The lower belly and underparts are white. (The amount of white is variable and in some instances covers most of the breast as well as the belly). The face, cheeks, ear coverts and chin are black. The wings and tail are grey/black, the outer edges of the flight and tail feathers are edged with crimson. The female is grey above and white below, with crimson edges to the flight and tail feathers. The eyes are dark brown, the bill is pinkish/red and the legs and feet are flesh pink. Resident.
Size 15 cms.

Red-billed Buffalo Weaver
(Bubalornis n

Distributed throughout much of the region favouring areas of acacia thornbush a savannah. A large weaver, usually encountered in small parties. During the bree season several pairs establish individual nesting chambers within a communal n of sticks placed high in an acacia or other suitable tree. The plumage appears ent black, but the basal section of much of the feathering is white, which shows whenever the plumage is disarranged. The primary and secondary flight feathers narrowly edged with white. The females and immature birds are browner than the males. The eyes are dark brown, the bill is bright red and the legs and feet are blackish. Resident. Size 25 cms.

White-billed Buffalo Weaver
(Bubalornis albiros

Found over much of the region in acacia woodlands and, like the Red-billed Buff Weaver (*Bubalornis niger*), has the plumage all black with white basal sections to feathers, which show when the plumage is ruffled. The outer edges of the primary and secondary flight feathers are white. The bill is white during the breeding seas becoming black at other times. The female is similar to the male but has a blackish bill at all times. The eyes are dark brown, the legs and feet are greyish/black. Resident. Size 25 cms.

White-headed Buffalo Weaver
(Dinemellia dinemer

A species found throughout much of the region in areas of dry bush and acacia scr and woodland. The head, neck, chin, throat, breast and belly are pure white. A sm black patch encircles the eye. The mantle, back and wing coverts are dusky brown The primary and secondary flight feathers are dark brown/black, boldly edged wit white. The rump and under tail coverts are bright red, being very conspicuous in flight. The tail is dark brown/black, narrowly edged with white. The eyes are dark brown, the bill, legs and feet are black. The sexes are alike. Resident. Size 23 cms.

White-browed Sparrow Weaver
(Plocepasser mah

Locally common throughout much of the region favouring areas of dry thornbush and scrub. The forehead, crown and face are dark brown, a broad white stripe extends from above the eye to the nape. The ear coverts, nape, mantle and wing coverts are earth brown. The chin, throat, breast, belly and underparts are pure white. They have a dark brown/black moustachial stripe which extends down the sides of the neck. The wing coverts are blackish, broadly edged with white, the primary and secondary flight feathers are dark brown/black. The rump is pure whit and the tail dark brown finely edged with white. The eyes are dark brown, the bill i black and the legs and feet are dull red. The sexes are alike. Resident. Size 15 cms.

Rufous-tailed Weaver
(Histurgops ruficaud

A species that occurs locally, mainly in northern Tanzania, being very common in areas of the Serengeti, particularly around Ndutu and Naabi Hill. A large weaver with the feathers of the head, mantle, back and wing coverts dark brown boldly edged with buff/grey. The chin, throat, breast, belly and flanks are grey/buff streake and spotted with dark brown. The primary and secondary flight feathers are dark brown and chestnut narrowly edged with buff. The central tail feathers are dark brown, the outer feathers are rich chestnut. The eyes are very pale blue, the bill is black and the legs and feet are greyish/black. The sexes are alike. Resident. Size 22 cms.

Grey-headed Social Weaver
(Pseudonigrita arn...

A small weaver encountered throughout much of the region in areas of dry scrub, light acacia woodland. The forehead and crown are pale grey, the remainder of the head, neck, mantle and the whole of the underside are grey/buff. The wing covers and inner portion of the secondary flight feathers are dark brown, the outer portion of the secondaries are grey/buff. The primary flight feathers are dark brown/black, the short tail is brown/black narrowly edged with buff. The eyes are dark brown, bill, legs and feet are blackish with a flush of dull red. The sexes are alike. Reside... Size 13 cms.

Speckle-fronted Weaver
(Sporopipes fron...

A very gregarious species found in areas of dry bush and scrub, woodland and cultivated farmland. The forehead and fore-crown are black, finely speckled with white, the hind-crown, nape and sides of the neck are rufous. The face, ear covert, chin, throat and underside are grey/white. They have a prominent black moustac... stripe. The mantle and wing coverts are ashy-brown, the primary and secondary flight feathers and the tail are dark brown edged with buff/grey. The eyes are dark brown, the bill, legs and feet are dull grey/black. The sexes are alike. Resident. Size 13 cms.

Rufous Sparrow
(Passer motiter...

A species favouring open acacia thornbush and light woodland as well as cultiva... farmland and human habitations. The male has the forehead and crown grey. A rufous band extends from the rear of the eyes around the ear coverts and the sides the neck, bordered along the front edge by a band of black. The chin and throat are black, the cheeks, breast, belly and underparts are white/grey. The back, rump and wing coverts are rufous streaked with black, the tail and primary and secondary flight feathers are dark brown edged with buff. The female has the chin and throat grey not black. The bill, legs and feet are blackish. Residents. Size 14 cms.

Grey-headed Sparrow
(Passer grise...

A common local resident over much of the region. The head and neck are grey, the chin, throat and upper breast are white merging to grey on the lower breast, belly a... underparts. The mantle, rump and wing coverts are grey/rufous, the primary and secondary flight feathers are earth brown edged with buff. The eyes are dark brown, the bill is black and the legs and feet are dull grey/red. The sexes are alike. Residen... Size 15 cms.

Yellow-spotted Petronia
(Petronia pyrgi...

Locally distributed in areas of dry bush and savannah as well as patches of cultivated farmland. The male has the head, neck and mantle plain grey, the chin and throat are white. a patch of pale yellow is present in the centre of the lower throat. They have a faint grey/buff eyebrow stripe. The breast, belly and underparts are grey/white. The tail and the primary and secondary flight feathers are dark brown edged with grey/white. The female is similar to the male but the yellow thro... spot is often very faint. The eyes are dark brown, the bill is buff/grey and the legs an... feet are grey/black. This species can easily be confused with the Yellow-throated Petronia (*Petronia superciliaris*) which has the upper-parts heavily streaked. Resident. Size 15 cms.

Cardinal Quelea
(Quelea card…

Locally common in areas of bush, scrub, grassland and cultivated farmland, establishing breeding colonies in marshy areas with dense rank vegetation. The … has the entire head, chin and throat bright crimson red. The breast, belly and underparts are creamy-white with some faint streaking on the flanks. The feathe… on the mantle, back, tail and wings is dark brown edged and streaked with tawny and buff. The female (illustrated) lacks the bright crimson plumage of the male, having the head buff, streaked with tawny and black and the chin and throat white/buff. The eyes are dark brown, the bill is black on the male and buff/grey o… the female. The legs and feet are dull red/pink. Resident. Size 10 cms.

Red-billed Quelea
(Quelea qu…

A very gregarious species often encountered in enormous flocks feeding in areas … bush, scrub, grassland and cultivated farmland where they can cause considerab… damage to crops. In breeding plumage the male usually has the forehead, face, ch… and throat black, although occasionally the head is rufous. The crown, nape, side… the neck and the breast are buff with a wash of pink, the belly and underparts are whitish. The feathers of the back, wings and tail have dark brown centres edged w… buff/white. The female (illustrated) has the head grey/brown finely streaked with dark brown and a buff/white eye stripe. Immature birds and males in non-breedin… plumage resemble females. The eyes are dark brown, the bill is bright red and the legs and feet are dull orange/yellow. Resident. Size 13 cms.

Red-collared Widowbird
(Euplectes ard…

Locally common throughout the region, encountered in areas of rank grassland, scrub and bush. In breeding plumage the male has a long flowing tail, the entire plumage being black with the exception of a broad scarlet breast band. In the highlands of Kenya, Tanzania and Uganda this species also has the crown, nape a… sides of the neck scarlet. The primary and secondary flight feathers are edged with buff/white. The female has the upper plumage dark brown boldly edged and streaked with tawny/buff. The chin and throat are yellowish/buff, the breast is buf… the belly and underparts white. In non-breeding plumage the male has similar plumage to the female but is larger and more heavily streaked above. The eyes are dark brown. The bill of the breeding male is black and at other times is buff/grey li… that of the female. The legs and feet are blackish. Resident. Size: Breeding male 28 cms, female 13 cms.

Yellow Bishop
(Euplectes capens…

Locally distributed throughout the region in areas of scrub, bush and rank vegetation. During the breeding season the male has predominantly black plumage with a bright yellow shoulder patch and loose bright yellow feathering on the rump… The primary and secondary flight feathers are edged with buff. The female has the upper feathering dark brown broadly edged with yellow/buff and the rump olive yellow finely streaked with brown. The underside is buff/white streaked with earth brown. During non-breeding periods the upper plumage of the male resembles that of the female. He is, however, larger, has a yellow rump, is more heavily streaked above and has darker wings and tail. The eyes are dark brown, The bill on the breeding male is blackish with some white on the lower mandible and on the femal… is grey/buff. The legs and feet are blackish. Resident. Size 15 cms.

Northern Red Bishop
(Euplectes franciscan…

A species with local distribution in Uganda and the Rift Valley in Kenya, frequentin… reedbeds and other areas of aquatic vegetation around the margins of lakes. The ma… in breeding plumage has the forehead, crown, upper face, breast and belly black. Th… nape, cheeks, neck, chin and throat are bright red. The mantle, wing coverts, under tail coverts and elongated upper tail coverts are also bright red. The tail and flight feathers are dark brown. The female has the upper feathering dark brown, broadly edged and streaked with buff, while the underside is buff/white with some faint streaking on the breast. Immature birds and males in non-breeding plumage resemble females. The eyes are dark brown, the bill is black and the legs and feet are dusky red. This species may be confused with the Southern Red Bishop (*Euplectes orix*) which is larger and has most of the crown bright red. Resident. Size 10 cms.

Jackson's Widowbird
(Euplectes jack...

A species of highland regions at elevations over 1500 metres in western and cent... Kenya and northern Tanzania. The male in breeding plumage has a long decurve... tail and almost entirely black feathering, the only exceptions being a yellow/bro... shoulder patch and the flight feathers having brown edges. Males are often seen displaying, leaping several feet into the air from deep grass. The female has the upper feathering dark brown boldly edged and streaked with buff. The underside... buff with darker streaking on the breast and flanks. In non-breeding plumage the male is similar to the female but is generally browner. The eyes are dark brown, th... bill of the breeding male is blue/grey, the bill of the female is yellow/grey. The le... and feet are black. Resident. Size: Breeding male 36 cms, female 14 cms.

Redwing Starling
(Onychognathus m...

Distributed over much of the region, favouring hill sides, rocky outcrops and gorges, woodlands and, in some areas, towns and cities. A large starling with a long tail, the ma... has glossy violet blue/black plumage with a trace of green on the cheeks. The primary flight feathers are rich chestnut tipped with black, the chestnut being most prominent when the bird is in flight. The plumage of the female is similar to that of the male but th... head, neck, chin, throat and upper breast are washed with dark grey and heavily streak... with black. They mate for life and, during the breeding season, can be encountered in pairs or small parties. Outside the breeding season flocks of several hundred have been recorded. The eyes are dark red/brown, the bill, legs and feet are black. Resident. Size 30 cms.

Bristle-crowned Starling
(Onychognathus salvado...

A bird mainly encountered in northern Kenya and north eastern Uganda, where they inhabit rocky hill sides and gorges as well as lake and riverside forests and woodlands. ... large starling with a very long, graduated tail. The male has glossy blue/black plumage with a wash of violet on the head and neck. A patch of raised, bristle-like feathers is present on the forehead which are noticeable even at a considerable distance. The prima... flight feathers are rich chestnut tipped with black, the chestnut being much more appare... in flight than when perched at rest. The female resembles the male but has a faint wash o... grey on the head and neck. The eyes are deep red, the slightly decurved bill is black and... the legs and feet are blackish. Resident. Size 40 cms.

Blue-eared Glossy Starling
(Lamprotornis chalyber...

A common and well distributed species throughout the region, inhabiting woodlands, lightly wooded savannahs, cultivated farmland and city parks and gardens. A robust starling with wonderful iridescent plumage, the colours of which change constantly as t... bird alters position in the strong african sunlight. The entire plumage is rich metallic blue/green, the crown, ear coverts, belly and underparts showing darker iridescent blue. The shoulders of the wings often show as violet patches and the tips of the wing coverts and the secondary flight feathers are boldly tipped with black. The eyes are golden yellov... the bill, legs and feet are black. The sexes are alike. Resident. Size 23 cms.

Ruppell's Long-tailed Glossy Starling
(Lamprotornis purpuropteru...

A common and conspicuous bird over much of the region in areas of open savannah... bush, scrub, cultivated farmland and human habitations. They are often common and very tame in the grounds of safari lodges and hotels. They are usually encountered in pairs or small parties. A large long-tailed Starling with striking iridescent plumage when viewed in bright sunlight, usually when seen in poor light... the entire plumage appears black. The head, neck, chin and throat are glossy black with a flush of metallic bronze. The nape, breast, belly, underparts and tail are metallic violet blue. The wing coverts and primary and secondary flight feathers are rich metallic green. Immature birds are duller than adults. The eyes are pale creamy-white, the bill, legs and feet are black. The sexes are alike. Resident. Size 36 cms.

Hildebrandt's Starling
(Spreo hildebr...

A bird of southern Kenya and northern Tanzania inhabiting areas of bush, lightl[y] wooded savannah and cultivated farmland, often being encountered in small flo[cks] foraging on the ground. A typical starling with very attractive plumage. The upperparts, wings and tail are a metallic blue, as are the chin, throat and upper breast. The tips of the wing coverts and the secondary flight feathers are black. T[he] lower breast, belly and underparts are rich chestnut/orange. The eyes are bright [red,] the bill, legs and feet are black. The sexes are alike. This species can easily be confused with the Superb Starling (*Spreo superbus*), which although similar has [a] narrow white breast band, white undertail coverts and creamy-white eyes. Resid[ent.] Size 18 cms.

Superb Starling
(Spreo super...

A small starling with stunning plumage, being a widespread and common specie[s] throughout much of the region. They are present in a wide range of habitats including lightly wooded savannahs, woodlands, areas of bush and scrub and human habitations. Common and usually extremely tame in the grounds of safar[i] lodges and hotels. The forehead, crown, face, chin and throat are black, the nape, mantle, wings and tail are metallic blue, often with a flush of green, particularly o[n] the wings. The tips of the wing coverts and the secondary flight feathers are black[.] The upper breast is blue/black and is separated from the chestnut/orange lower breast and belly by a narrow band of white. The undertail coverts are white. The e[yes] are creamy-white, the bill, legs and feet are black. The sexes are alike. Immature birds show little of the narrow white breast band, are generally duller and have da[rk] brown eyes. This species can easily be confused with Hildebrandt's Starling (*Spre[o] hildebrandti*) which lacks the narrow white breast band, has chestnut/orange undertail coverts and bright red eyes. Resident. Size 18 cms.

Golden-breasted Starling
(Cosmopsarus reg...

This species is possibly the most beautiful of the starlings found in East Africa. A slender, long-tailed bird encountered over much of the region, frequenting areas o[f] dry thornbush and scrub. A rather shy and wary species. The forehead, crown, na[pe] and neck are iridescent metallic green, the chin, throat and cheeks are metallic blu[e.] The upper breast is metallic purple, the remainder of the breast, belly and underparts are rich golden yellow. The mantle, rump and wings are deep metallic blue, washed with purple. The long graduated tail is violet blue with a strong wash[?] of bronze. The eyes are creamy-white, the bill, legs and feet are black. The sexes ar[e] alike. Immature birds are duller than adults. Resident. Size 36 cms.

Ashy Starling
(Cosmopsarus unicol...

A locally common species in areas of acacia woodland and lightly wooded grasslands, particularly in the vicinity of baobab trees. There are many in and around Tarangire National Park in Tanzania. Compared with other starling specie[s] the region, the Ashy Starling has rather dull plumage, being almost uniform ashy-brown. The cheeks, chin, throat and the primary and secondary flight feathers are usually a slightly darker brown and the very long graduated tail often shows faint vermiculations. The eyes are pale yellow, the bill, legs and feet are black. Immature birds are usually greyer than adults. The sexes are alike. Resident. Size 30 cms.

Wattled Starling
(Creatophora cinere...

A common and widely distributed species throughout the region, occurring in area[s] of open grassland, bush and scrub and acacia woodlands. They are very gregarious and often associate with plains game animals, feeding on the insects disturbed by the grazing herds. The head, neck, mantle and the whole of the underside are light grey. The wing coverts are light grey at the base and white at the tips, the primary an[d] secondary flight feathers and the tail are black. The rump is white. In breeding plumage the male has a patch of bright yellow skin covering the ear coverts and extending around the eye to the back of the crown. The front of the head, face and chin are black, with large black wattles on the forehead, crown and throat. During periods of non-breeding the wattles disappear, being replaced by grey and black feathering. The eyes are dark brown, the bill, legs and feet are dull flesh pink. The female is similar to the male in non-breeding plumage. Resident. Size 21 cms.

Red-billed Oxpecker
(Buphagus erythorhyr

Locally common throughout much of East Africa in areas of open grassland, bus
and scrub and light woodlands. They are particularly numerous on the open pla
where they associate with herds of plains game, feeding by climbing all over the
animals picking off ticks and other blood sucking insects. The head, neck, wings
rump and tail are earth-brown, the breast, belly and underparts are buff. The eye
bright red, surrounded by a bright yellow orbital ring. The bill is bright red, the l
and feet are black. The sexes are alike. This species may be confused with the
Yellow-billed Oxpecker (*Buphagus africanus*) which has a bright yellow base to
bill and a pale buff rump. Resident. Size 18 cms.

Yellow-billed Oxpecker
(Buphagus africa

Widely distributed throughout the region frequenting areas of open grasslands a
light bush and scrub. Like the Red-billed Oxpecker (*Buphagus erythorhynchus*)
species is dependent on large herds of plains game or domestic stock, feeding on
range of ticks and other blood sucking insects that they pluck from the animal hi
The head, neck, wings and tail are dark brown, the rump is pale buff. The breast,
belly and underparts are buff/brown. The eyes are bright red, the bill is bright ye
at the base and red at the tip, the legs and feet are black. The sexes are alike. This
species may be confused with the Red-billed Oxpecker (*Buphagus erythorhynch*
which has an all red bill, a darker rump and a bright yellow orbital ring. Resident.
Size 19 cms.

Black-headed Oriole
(Oriolus larva

A common species found in forests, woodlands and areas of bush and scrub. The
head, neck, chin, throat and upper breast are black. The mantle, lower breast, bell
and underparts are bright chrome yellow, the wing coverts are olive yellow and th
primary and secondary flight feathers are black edged with yellow and white. The
central tail feathers are olive yellow, the outer tail feathers are golden yellow. The
eyes and the bill are deep red, the legs and feet are blackish. Immature birds have
yellow streaking on the head and some black streaking on the breast. The sexes are
alike. Resident. Size 23 cms.

Drongo
(Dicrurus adsimi

A common species throughout the region, inhabiting a wide range of habitat types
including woodlands, areas of scrub and bush, lightly wooded savannahs and park
and gardens. They can often be seen perched on a branch overlooking a clearing
from where they hawk for insects which they capture in mid-flight. The entire
plumage is glossy black, with a hint of brown on the edges of the primary and
secondary flight feathers. The long, broad tail is deeply forked, less so in the female
The eyes are deep red, the bill, legs and feet are black. The sexes are alike. Resident
Size 25 cms.

Square-tailed Drongo
(Dicrurus ludwig

Widely distributed but locally common throughout much of East Africa. A bird of
dense forests and woodlands, often seen hawking for insects from a perch
overlooking a forest clearing. The entire plumage is glossy black which, under som
lighting conditions shows a flush of deep blue. The tail is shorter than that of the
Drongo (*Dicrurus adsimilis*) and lacks the deep fork, being almost square. The eyes
are dark brown and the bill, legs and feet are black. The female is generally duller in
appearance than the male. Resident. Size 18 cms.

Pied Crow
(Corvus a...

A locally distributed but common species in East Africa, being found in a wide variety of habitat types including open grasslands, lake and river edges, cultivate farmland and towns and cities. The head, throat and upper breast are glossy blac the mantle, the sides of the neck and the lower breast are white. The belly, underparts, wings and tail are glossy black. The eyes are dark brown, the legs and feet are black. The sexes are alike. Resident. Size 46 cms.

White-necked Raven
(Corvus albic...

A bird encountered on rocky slopes, on hill sides, in gorges and in the vicinity of human habitations, where they perform the role of scavenger. With the exception a broad white crescent-shaped band on the hind-neck, the entire plumage is gloss blue/black. The eyes are dark brown, the large, thick bill is black with a white tip. The legs and feet are black. The sexes are alike, although the female has a smaller bill. Resident. Size 56 cms.

Fan-tailed Raven
(Corvus rhipidu...

A common species around inland cliffs, gorges and hill sides in northern Kenya, northern Uganda and Somalia. They are often quite common and reasonably tame and around safari lodges. The entire plumage is glossy black often showing a purp or blue iridescence, particularly on the wings. When the bird is at rest the folded wings extend 2 to 3 cms beyond the end of the short tail. The eyes are dark brown, the bill, legs and feet are black. Immature birds are duller in appearance than adult birds. The sexes are alike. Resident. Size 46 cms.

Cape Rook
(Corvus capen...

A slender built crow, widely distributed in East Africa, favouring areas of open plains and grasslands, cultivated farmland, pastures and human habitations. The plumage is entirely black which, if viewed in good light, often has a sheen of blue and bronze. The black bill is, for a crow at least, long and slender. The eyes are dark brown, the legs and feet are black. Immature birds are often duller and have a browner appearance than do the adults. The sexes are alike. Resident. Size 43 cms.

Indian House Crow
(Corvus splender...

A species introduced from Asia towards the end of the nineteenth century, which is now well established and quite numerous in the coastal regions of Kenya and Tanzania. The hind-crown, neck and breast are dusky-grey, the upper plumage is glossy blue/black with a sheen of purple on the wings. The belly and underparts are blue/black with a wash of grey. The eyes are dark brown, the bill, legs and feet are black. Immature birds lack the plumage gloss of the adults. The sexes are alike. Resident. Size 33 cms.

Piapiac
(Ptilostomus afer

A bird of western and northern Uganda, usually encountered in small flocks on grasslands and pastures, where they associate with large game animals and domesti stock, feeding on the insects disturbed by the grazing herds. The plumage in mainly black with a wash of brown on the wings and the long graduated tail. The eyes are dark brown, the bill, legs and feet are black. The sexes are alike. Resident. Size 35 cms.

INDEX